Spiritual Protection

*The Ultimate Guide to Psychic Self-Defense
and Kundalini Yoga*

Your Free Gift
(only available for a limited time)

Thanks for getting this book! If you want to learn more about various spirituality topics, then join Mari Silva's community and get a free guided meditation MP3 for awakening your third eye. This guided meditation mp3 is designed to open and strengthen ones third eye so you can experience a higher state of consciousness. Simply visit the link below the image to get started.

https://spiritualityspot.com/meditation

Or, Scan the QR code!

Table of Contents

Part 1: Psychic Protection

The Spiritual Self-Defense Guide to Angelic Protection, Karma, Soul Cleansing, Aura Healing, and Defending Against Negative Energy

Introduction

People communicate with each other's energies all the time. Setting boundaries for energetic communication can be challenging. However, protecting yourself from other people's energies is critical to maintaining your energetic balance and a healthy mental state. Some people are more sensitive to others' vibes and have difficulty separating themselves from the energetic influences affecting them. They can pick up people's emotions more easily, which affects them. However, even if you do not belong to this category, stress, fatigue, and the lack of boundaries can make you more vulnerable to negative influences and psychic attacks. Either way, it doesn't hurt to consciously protect yourself from energetic effects.

Psychic connections can be beneficial. For example, they can help you bond in relationships or help you better understand how you relate to others and yourself as a person. However, it is unhealthy to allow people who aren't close to you or wish you harm to impact your vibes. Even if their emotions and vibes are positive, sometimes, you merely want to be aware of your feelings. Being self-aware is critical to understanding why you have specific sentiments. You cannot achieve this if you're always affected by other people's energies. Let's say you're in a good place emotionally but spend time with a friend going through a rough time. You'll feel the effects of their negative vibes and may have trouble separating your emotions from theirs.

Psychic protection can help you separate other people's feelings and thoughts from yours. For those more sensitive (temporarily or permanently) to others' energies, picking up their feelings is as easy as catching a cold. Learning to barricade your feelings will help you identify other people's vibes, filter these feelings, or block them if needed.

This book introduces you to setting psychic boundaries and creating a safe space for your emotions. Through practical exercises, you'll better understand who you are and how others' energies affect you. They will help you center and ground yourself to ward off and release unwanted influences. Paying attention to your chakras and auras is crucial to containing your energy and establishing psychic boundaries.

After emphasizing the importance of psychic protection, this book teaches you how to prepare your psyche by providing tips and exercises to raise your vibration and sharpen your psychic skills. You'll be provided plenty of techniques, cleansing rituals, and instructions for thoroughly cleansing your soul. Moreover, the book includes several simple cleansing rituals and methods for clearing your space and those around you. Once cleaned, you must heal your aura and reverse previous damage.

Several chapters are dedicated to different tools you can use for psychic protection. First, you learn to summon your guardian angels or an archangel to ask for their protection from psychic attacks. Then, you'll master the art of using protective crystals, plants, and symbols for protection. Also, you are taught how to use spells to defend against curses, hexes, and unwanted links, attachments, or relationships. Lastly, this book offers plenty of user-friendly ways to protect yourself at home or work, ward off negative vibes from your home, and protect your loved ones, pets, or children - whether they're near you or far away.

Chapter 1: Why Do We Need Psychic Protection?

Encounters with other people can lead to energy contamination.

When starting on the spiritual self-defense journey, many people ask why psychic protection is necessary. This question most often arises when performing rituals, including the manifestation of energy, emphasizing protection even when the ritual is for love, money, or healing. Mundane people wonder why this protection is needed, what dangers exist, and whether psychic attacks are so dangerous they require proper protection. However, there are no simple answers to these questions. You must first grasp the concept of energy and how it affects you to understand why you need protection from the unseen.

Consider this. During the day, you engage with multiple people, whether at home, grocery shopping, or just walking down the street. Each person has an energy aura, which directly affects their energy field. When you engage with these people, you're bound to be affected by their emotional state and energy. Your interactions with others create emotional connections, a natural aspect of being human, and whether you're aware of it or not, these emotional connections negatively affect you. Of course, this isn't to say all interactions can negatively affect your energy, but only those with harmful projections.

According to the laws of physics, everything in the world is made up of energy in motion, including your existence. So, in this context, your daily encounters with other people, whether family, friends, colleagues, or random strangers, are essentially the meeting of energetic bodies. This encounter leads to energy contamination. Indeed, you cannot see this energy, just as you can't see germs with your naked eye, but it doesn't make the fact that germs exist any less accurate. Energy permeates everything around you.

For instance, emotions are energy. Have you ever walked into a room where two people have just finished a heated argument, and you felt the tension and heavy atmosphere without being aware of the situation? This feeling of discomfort and agitation is normal. Even if you don't possess psychic abilities, your body will still react to invisible stimuli. They can influence your mood, stress levels, and overall well-being.

Another example of how energy affects your thoughts and emotions is when you meet someone for the first time and feel instantly drawn to them, or conversely, feel discomfort or unease. What do you think this initial impression is? Or, as youngsters say, what do you think a person's vibes are? They're the energetic connection between you and the other person. Similarly, if you've had a gut feeling about something and later found out your intuition was right, this intuitive response results from energy sensing it, even if you cannot see it.

Energy comes in many forms (discussed later in the chapter), but you must be especially careful when dealing with negative energy. Negative energies and psychic attacks are energy harmfully affecting you. Negative energy can be derived from many sources, including the environment, objects, or people with negative emotions or intentions. If you're exposed to this energy for long periods, it can be mentally and physically draining. On the other hand, psychic attacks are intentional and always direct energy attacks from one person to another. Although the intention behind these attacks can range from mild annoyance to fully-fledged hatred, they manifest in various ways, like nightmares, sudden illness, mental drain, or inexplicable dread or anxiety.

The need for psychic protection doesn't always stem from apparent danger, but it remains crucial, nonetheless. Many people misunderstand the need for psychic protection only when there's an evil spirit to ward off or a need to defend themselves against known attacks from their detractors. However, potential threats can take on many forms, and it's always best to be prepared for them. Psychic attacks are much like curses, except they don't require ritual magic tools. However, the impact is pretty much the same, i.e., devastating. People who practice psychic attacks don't need to rely on candles, symbols, altars, or rituals but instead manifest their negative energy and intuition to bring harm, suffering, or misfortune to their victim.

Therefore, psychic protection should be an absolute essential, especially for those involved in energy work or spiritual magic. Everything is made up of energy, meaning your energy fields interact with those around you continuously, making you vulnerable to negative energies and psychic attacks. These can severely affect your physical, emotional, and mental well-being. Psychic protection will come in handy; it acts as your shield against these negative forces and allows you to maintain a positive state of mind. Regular protection techniques like grounding, visualization, and cleansing strengthen your energetic boundaries and increase your resilience to negative energies, allowing you to navigate life with greater ease and positivity.

Understanding Energy

In the context of psychic protection and energy work, energy refers to the life force that permeates everything in the universe, tangible and intangible. It is the invisible force flowing within and around you, shaping your experiences and interactions with the world. This energy is neither good nor bad; it simply is. It can be positive or negative, depending on how it is harnessed and utilized. In energy work, practitioners aim to tap into this force and manipulate it to achieve specific outcomes, such as healing, manifestation, or psychic protection. Understanding the nature of energy and how it interacts with your energetic fields is crucial if you plan to engage in energy work or psychic protection. There are different energies, including:

1. **Personal Energy:** The energy generated and emitted from your body. It is influenced by your thoughts, emotions, and physical state and can be felt by others in your immediate vicinity.

2. **Environmental Energy:** This refers to energy in the physical environment around you. It can be influenced by factors such as the weather, geographical location, and human activity.

3. **Universal Energy:** The energy that exists throughout the universe and is often associated with spiritual or metaphysical beliefs. It is the source of all life and the driving force behind many natural phenomena.

4. **Vibrational Energy:** The frequency or vibration of energy, positive or negative. Higher vibrational energies, such as love and joy, benefit your well-being, while lower vibrational energies, such as fear and anger, negatively impact your mental, emotional, and physical health.

5. **Elemental Energy:** The energy associated with earth, air, fire, and water elements. It is often used in rituals and spells and has specific properties and associations that can be harnessed for different purposes.

Energy-Work Exercises

Do some energy work exercises to better understand and feel the energy surrounding you. Energy manipulation is defined as the practice of directing and manipulating the energy flow within and around you. This energy should be considered a force that permeates all things and can be accessed and used through many techniques and practices. Different energies can be manipulated, including spiritual, emotional, and physical.

Spiritual energy is the energy present in the universe and connects all things. Emotional energy is the energy we generate through emotions and feelings. Physical energy is the energy that powers your body and keeps you alive.

Energy manipulation uses various techniques to increase, direct, or remove energy. Some of these techniques include visualization, meditation, breathwork, and movement. By practicing energy manipulation, individuals can learn to balance and enhance their energy levels, clear blockages, and promote healing. Energy manipulation can be used for manifestation, and manifestation techniques are based on the idea that everything is made up of energy, including thoughts and emotions. By focusing your thoughts and intentions, you can direct the energy flow toward a specific goal or outcome, including manifesting abundance, success, love, and happiness.

Below are some techniques to manifest and manipulate energy:

• Creating an Energy Ball

To create a ball of energy, follow these steps:

1. Sit or stand comfortably in a quiet, relaxed environment. Close your eyes and take a few deep breaths to center yourself.

2. Visualize a ball of light in the center of your body, just below your navel. This ball can be any color, but many visualize it as white or gold.

3. As you inhale, imagine you are drawing energy up from the earth and into your body, filling the ball with energy. As you exhale, imagine the ball expanding and growing brighter.

4. Continue to breathe and visualize the energy ball growing larger and brighter. You might feel a tingling or warmth in your hands.

5. Once the ball of energy is large enough, you can direct it to a specific area or use it for healing, protection, or manifestation.

• Energy Sensing Exercise

The energy-sensing exercise is designed to help you become more aware of the energy around and within you. To do this exercise, follow these steps:

1. Find a space where you can sit comfortably and without interruption. This space can be indoors or outdoors, but ensure you have privacy and won't be disturbed.

2. Close your eyes and take a few deep breaths to relax your body and quiet your mind. If you have tension in your body, consciously release it as you exhale.

3. Once you are relaxed, bring your attention to the sensations in your body. Notice any physical sensations, such as tingling, warmth, or pressure. Don't judge or analyze the sensations. Simply observe them.

4. Gradually expand your awareness to include the space around your body. Notice any changes in the sensations. You may feel a shift in energy or a sense of expansion.

5. With your expanded awareness, tune into the energy around you. You could feel a subtle vibration or hum or sense a particular quality or color of energy. Pay attention to the impressions you receive.

6. Scan your body from head to toe, noticing the areas where you feel a change in energy. You may feel areas of tension or blockage or openness and flow.

7. Bring your attention back to your breath and take a few more deep breaths. Notice how you feel after this exercise. You should feel more grounded, centered, and connected to the energy around you.

Remember, this exercise is not about achieving a specific outcome; it's about cultivating your energy awareness and ability to sense it. With practice, you will sense energy more easily and accurately.

• **Energy Projection**

Energy projection intentionally sends energy from your body to a specific target or area. This projection can be used for various purposes, such as healing, protection, or manifestation. Here's a step-by-step guide for an energy projection exercise:

1. Find a quiet and comfortable space where you won't be disturbed. Sit or stand comfortably with your feet firmly on the ground.

2. Close your eyes and take a few deep breaths, allowing yourself to relax and let go of the tension or stress in your body.

3. Visualize a ball of bright, white light in the center of your body, just below your belly button. This ball of light represents your energy and power.

4. Focus your attention on the body area where you feel the most energy or sensation. It could be your hands, your chest, or your forehead.

5. Consciously direct your energy to that area by imagining the ball of light expanding and filling that space.

6. Once you feel a strong connection to that area, imagine directing the energy outward toward your intended target, a person, a place, or an object.

7. Visualize a beam of light extending from your body to the target, carrying your energy.

8. Keep focusing on the target and visualize your energy being received and absorbed by the target.

9. When you feel ready, slowly bring your awareness back to your body and the ball of light in your center.

10. Take a few deep breaths, and when you're ready, slowly open your eyes.

Remember, always use energy projection with positive intentions and respect for others. Also, grounding yourself afterward to release excess energy and return to a state of balance is important.

• Energy Shielding

Energy shielding is a technique using your energy to create a protective shield around yourself. This shield can help you to ward off negative energy or influences from others and promote a sense of safety and security. Here's a step-by-step guide for an energy shielding exercise:

1. Find a quiet and comfortable space where you won't be disturbed. Sit or stand comfortably with your feet firmly on the ground.

2. Close your eyes and take a few deep breaths, allowing yourself to relax and let go of the tension or stress in your body.

3. Visualize a ball of bright, white light in the center of your body, just below your belly button. This ball of light represents your energy and power.

4. Imagine this ball of light expanding and surrounding your body like a protective bubble. See it getting larger and stronger with each breath you take.

5. Set an intention for your energy shield. You can use a simple statement or affirmation, such as *"I am protected and safe from negative energy or influences."*

6. As you continue to visualize your energy shield, focus on the safety and protection it provides. You may feel warmth, peace, or

calmness.

7. If you sense negative energy or unwanted influences trying to enter your energy shield, simply visualize them bouncing off and returning to the universe.

8. When you're ready to end the shielding practice, slowly bring your awareness back to your body and the ball of light in your center.

9. Take a few deep breaths, and when you're ready, slowly open your eyes.

You can experiment with different colors, shapes, and sizes for your energy shield or program it with a specific intention or purpose.

Why You Need Psychic Protection

There's no shortage of negativity in this world and numerous ways for this negative energy to reach you. Therefore, psychic protection is essential to maintain a healthy and balanced energy field. Whether the negative energies affecting you are intentional or unintentional, they can have a detrimental effect on your overall well-being. Psychic protection is particularly important for people sensitive to energy, like empaths or psychics, because they are more susceptible to absorbing the negative energies from their environment. Here's why it's essential to have psychic protection for yourself and your family:

1. Physical Harm

Properly utilizing techniques to manifest protection energy can help safeguard you against physical harm and other threats posed by psychic attacks. However, this doesn't mean psychic protection can deflect physical attacks. Instead, it's a more subtle manner of guiding you out of harm's way. Protection magic equips you with intuitive guidance to protect you from potential threats. When you utilize psychic protection, you may not even realize when you're saved from dangerous situations.

2. Harmful Energy

Harmful energy is derived from the unconscious remnants of day-to-day living, for instance, sadness, arguments, anger, or illness. This energy can cause physical, emotional, and mental discomfort, but most people don't notice because they're used to feeling this way. When using psychic protection, you'll stay protected from this harmful energy that drains your energy and dulls your mood.

3. Harmful Judgments

Thoughts are powerful forms of energy manifesting real consequences, even if they're not physically present. When you judge or project negative thoughts onto another person, you could harm them psychically and vice versa. While judging or comparing people is natural, the intention behind your thoughts is important. When people condemn or even name-call or hate someone, they are psychically attacking them. So, you should be mindful of your words and thoughts toward others. The same goes for other people, but since you can't control their thoughts, practicing psychic protection techniques is best to protect yourself from their harmful judgment (discussed in detail in the following chapters).

4. Psychic Vampires

You've probably encountered the term "psychic vampire" at least once. This term refers to someone who drains other people's energy without realizing what they're doing. These people are not self-aware or consider the negative effect they have on others. Psychic vampires often have mental, emotional, or physical issues, so they seek out those who burn brightly and feed on their energies. However, this behavior only brings them down further, and ultimately, they become shunned by others. Using techniques to protect you psychically can help protect you from being drained by psychic vampires.

5. Mesmerism

Mesmerism is a psychic attack suppressing an individual's will, caused by charming and convincing them with hypnotic effects. It is a mind control similar to brainwashing and is often unintentional or seen as harmless by the mesmerist. However, when an individual's discernment and intuition are suspended, it can be damaging. Some metaphysicians explain that the mesmerist projects vital life force, such as prana or akasha, from their eyes to charm, seduce, and control the target. The mesmerism's energy is soft and seductive to enrapture the victim. Psychic protection comes in handy when dealing with mesmeric individuals.

6. Past Life Energies

Some believe that negative energies can attach to the soul and follow from one life to the next until an underlying issue is confronted and resolved. These energies can be present from birth or activated when a similar situation in the current life is encountered. Where a person was cursed in a past life, that curse or its residual patterns are carried into their present existence. It can be challenging to differentiate between the effects of your karma and past-life curses, but you can work toward resolving them through deep reflection, meditation, and self-awareness.

7. Yourself

In psychic practice, your well-being can sometimes be compromised by your actions or lack thereof. Low self-esteem, a lack of awareness, distorted boundaries, unresolved emotions, personal fears, and critical self-judgments can contribute to psychic attack scenarios. Fearful individuals might see malevolent entities lurking in the shadows, while angry people see everyone as hostile and seeking to do them harm. The world around you is a mirror, and you inadvertently become your own enemy, sabotaging yourself. Rather than placing blame elsewhere, it is important to introspect, realize you could be involved, and take responsibility for your actions.

Psychic protection is an essential aspect of spiritual practice and everyday life. The world is filled with different energies, and not all are positive. Your thoughts, emotions, and interactions with others can leave you vulnerable to harmful energies manifesting as physical, mental, or emotional discomfort. Therefore, protecting yourself from negative energies is crucial to maintaining your well-being and living a balanced life.

Chapter 2: Prepare Your Psyche First

Now that you understand the significance of psychic protection and negative energies' impact on your life, take the first step to protect yourself against these vibes. However, before you start, you must prepare your psyche first. This chapter covers multiple techniques to raise your vibration and sharpen your psychic skills to prepare for various cleansing and protection rituals.

Raising Your Vibrations

Taking yoga classes can help raise your vibration.
https://pixabav.com/sv/photos/yoga-utomhus-soluppg%C3%A5ng-meditation-6723315/

The energy particles in your body are constantly moving and vibrating at a specific rhythm. Your mood and mindset impact the frequency of your vibrations. Positive emotions like gratitude, happiness, and peacefulness can raise your vibes, while negative ones like fear, anxiety, and anger lower their frequency. In other words, attracting positivity into your life increases your vibrations. You will feel lighter spiritually, emotionally, and physically when you vibrate at a higher frequency, while low vibes make you feel heavy and stressed.

Sometimes, it can be hard to control your emotions, especially if your work or home life is stressful. However, a few things can calm your thoughts, relax your body to attract positive vibes and connect you with everything and everyone in the universe.

Move Your Body

You have probably heard about the many benefits of working out, walking, and yoga, but do you know they can raise your vibrations? Moving your body increases the levels of chemicals like dopamine, serotonin, and endorphins helping you to relax and improve your mood. Moving your body reduces harmful hormones like cortisol and adrenaline that make you stressed and anxious.

You don't have to do intense exercises or go to the gym daily; swimming, dancing, riding a bike, walking in nature, hula hooping, jumping a rope, or taking a yoga class will do the trick. It doesn't matter what you do as long as you constantly move your body.

Listen to Music

Everyone knows music makes you feel good and improves your mood. Listen to songs that energize and uplift you while getting ready in the morning or on your way to work. Sing along or dance to the music, and you will feel your vibes rising.

Repeat Affirmations

Affirmations are positive statements that influence your subconscious and conscious mind to think positively. Repeating affirmations can alter your mood, change your mindset, and boost your confidence. However, they will only work if you believe in yourself and what you say and repeat them daily.

Create your own affirmations or repeat these statements to raise your vibrations.

- I am a highly vibrational human.

- I feel at peace.
- I am full of energy.
- I am a magnet that only attracts positive vibes.
- I am thankful to be healthy.
- I am raising my vibration.
- I create my life.
- I love the person I have become.
- I am surrounded by positivity.
- I vibrate higher and feel lighter.
- I embrace all the high-vibe experiences coming my way.
- I am grateful and happy with my life.
- I am vibrating at a high frequency.
- I choose gratitude and happiness every day.
- I am in harmony with the universe.
- I deserve all the good things in life.
- I choose gratitude and joy every day.
- I choose to love and have positive energy.
- I am in control of my life.
- I am raising my vibes.
- I attract positive experiences and people.
- I only think positively.
- I give joy and receive positivity and happiness.
- I witness miracles every day.
- I have everything I need.
- I spread positivity wherever I go.
- I manifest my desires through my high vibrations.
- I choose to raise my vibes every day.

Aromatherapy

Aromatherapy is using essential oils to improve your well-being and health. It is an ancient holistic treatment people still use today. Some scents can impact your brain and influence your emotions. For instance, smelling lavender oil can relax you and reduce stress. Frankincense, chamomile, and eucalyptus are known for their calming effects. Smelling citrus and peppermint can improve your mood and raise your vibration.

You can use an oil diffuser to spread the scent in your home, apply diluted oils on your wrists or behind your earlobe, or use scented candles in the room where you are.

Daily Routine

Many people associate having a daily routine with boredom, but it can be effective in raising your vibration. If you set time aside each day to do something you enjoy, you will have something to look forward to. For example, morning coffee or walking in nature can be great choices. Be sure to incorporate things that bring joy into your daily routine. Even if it's something small like eating chocolate, it will make your day extra special.

Plants

Bring nature into your home if you don't have a garden or live away from nature. Place a few plant pots in different areas in your house. They will improve the décor, reduce stress, make you feel relaxed, clean the air, improve your mood, and raise your vibration.

Journaling

Many thoughts go through your head that can cause stress and anxiety and lower your vibrations. Putting these thoughts on paper is a great way to clear your head and come face-to-face with whatever is troubling you. Often, when you write down your fears and read them out loud, you will realize they aren't as serious as your mind has made them out to be.

Every night before you go to sleep, sit down and write every thought in your journal, whether these are issues you are dealing with or goals you wish to achieve. Organize and prioritize them, and develop a plan to solve your problems or accomplish your goals.

If you are new to journaling and looking for things to write to raise your vibration, tackle these questions:

- How can you add value to your life and the world?
- What nourishes your body, mind, and spirit?
- How do you practice self-love and self-care?
- What makes you get up in the morning and why?
- What makes you the proudest?
- When and where do you feel happiest?
- Describe your ideal day and what you can do to achieve this feeling.

Practice Gratitude

Being grateful for your blessings and focusing on what you have rather than what's missing can change your outlook and raise your vibration. Practicing gratitude can be challenging for some as they struggle to find things to be grateful for every day. However life is full of many gifts you can be thankful for, but they are usually small things you often don't notice or you take for granted, like not facing traffic on your way to work, having a perfect cup of coffee, or getting a hug from your neighbor's dog.

Write down the things you are thankful for, but instead of making a list like "I am grateful for my children" or "I am grateful for my health," explain why you appreciate them, what makes them special, how they make your life better, and how you would feel without them. Daily, write one thing you are grateful for with three to five reasons why they are significant. By the time you have finished, you will feel better, and your vibes will rise. Whenever you feel low, you can always turn to your gratitude journal to remember all your blessings, and your mood will instantly change.

Socialize

Even the most introverted people need to connect with others and feel part of a community; it's human nature. Spend time with people who lift you up and make you feel better about yourself. Choose ones you share common interests and values with and can talk to about anything. Stay away from people who lower your vibes by judging you, making you feel bad about yourself, and reminding you of your past failures rather than supporting and celebrating your successes. Look at your circle and notice who raises your energy after spending time with them and who brings you down and drains you. Positivity is infectious, so surround yourself with people from whom you can catch positive vibes.

Reiki

Reiki is a healing technique where a practitioner uses their hand to transfer positive energy to your body to reduce stress and make you feel relaxed. During a reiki session, the practitioner will loosen negative energy and clear your pathways to raise vibrations.

Disconnect

In this modern age, people are always online and behind their screens, usually checking their friends and family's pictures on Instagram, and can't help but compare their lives with those of their friends. It leads to negative thoughts and low vibes. Disconnect for a few hours every day and connect with yourself. Do something you love and practice self-care, like a massage, reading a book, cooking a healthy meal, trying something new, or finishing a project you have been procrastinating on. Simply slow down, focus on the present, and enjoy the moment.

Be Creative

When was the last time you did a creative project? Unfortunately, many people don't have the time to create or have been discouraged. Do something you are passionate about to spend hours on and lose yourself in it. You will feel less stressed, more confident, and in a better mood after you finish. These feelings usually result from dopamine released in your body when you feel accomplished and proud of something you created.

If you can't find something you are passionate about, think back to your childhood. What did you enjoy doing? Or maybe there is something you have always wanted to try, like painting, singing, or writing. When you find it, start creating.

Be in Nature

Nature is the closest thing humans have to magic. Walking or hiking while being surrounded by beautiful scenery can alter your mood and vibes. The sunlight on your face, the wind in your hair, and the ground beneath your feet can make you feel relaxed and at peace.

Declutter

Nothing says low vibration more than clutter. Messy environments drain your energy and make you feel stressed and uncomfortable. Many of these unnecessary items can carry negative energies or memories to make you unhappy. Remove everything you no longer need to allow easy energy flow in your home. Keep what you use, make yourself happy, and add meaning to your life. Donate your clutter instead of throwing it away, making this process more meaningful.

Get to the Root of the Negativity

Dig deep into yourself to determine the reason behind the negative energy and emotions you have been experiencing. Journaling and therapy can push you to get real with yourself, confront your feelings to get to the root of your problem, fix it, and raise your vibes.

Love Yourself

Treat yourself with love and compassion. Use positive words when you talk about yourself, and avoid negative thoughts. Imagine a loved one feeling low and coming to you for support. What would you tell them?

Use this same kindness on yourself whenever you feel sad and need encouragement.

Forgive and Forget

Holding grudges can make you feel heavy, consume you with negative emotions, and lower your vibes. It's time to forgive and forget. Either forgive the ones who hurt you and turn over a new leaf or let them go and move on from everything they put you through, releasing the negative energy and replacing it with positive energy.

What matters the most is forgiving yourself. Don't spend your life in regrets and self-blame. Understand you are human, and making mistakes is normal; it's how you learn.

Meditation

Meditation is one of the most effective tools against low vibes. It looks inward and focuses on positive emotions and letting go of the chaos and negative energy impacting your vibration. Meditation is like decluttering your brain and spirit as you let go of the thoughts and emotions no longer benefiting you and embrace positive and calming ones. You can meditate at home after you wake up, before bed, or even at work. You only need ten or fifteen minutes daily, making a huge difference in your life.

Meditation Technique
Instructions:

1. Choose a quiet room or space with no distractions, and set your phone to silent. You can play soft music if you prefer.
2. Sit straight, place your hands on your knees with your palms facing up, and ensure you are comfortable.
3. Close your eyes, clear your mind, and focus on the present moment.
4. Breathe deeply through your nose and out through your mouth a few times.
5. Feel the stress, anxiety, and negativity leave your body with every breath you take and exhale.
6. Focus on your breathing and feel the air entering and leaving your chest. You are inhaling positivity and relaxation and exhaling negative vibes.

7. Visualize yourself surrounded by white light. This light is the calming, loving, and healing energy raising your vibration.

8. Feel the light nourish and energize your body, mind, and spirit with every breath.

9. Feel positive emotions like love, joy, gratitude, kindness, compassion, or other feelings you experience in that moment.

10. Sit with these feelings for a while, then end the session by expressing gratitude.

Visualization

Visualizing is imagining something you want to attract into your life. Even though you only visualize the moment and aren't living it, you can still experience all its positive emotions.

Visualization Technique

Instructions:

1. Sit or lie in a quiet room, whatever makes you comfortable.

2. Close your eyes and slowly breathe until you feel relaxed and calm.

3. Visualize a moment or a place that makes you happy. It can also be a place you hope to visit.

4. Experience the moment in your imagination with each of your five senses. Focus on what you hear, like your mother's or children's voices. Focus on the scents around you, like flowers, your grandma's favorite recipe, or the ocean. What are you feeling? Is it a cold winter night or a warm summer day? Look around your image and take in everything you see, like the stars, moon, flowers, or your loved ones' faces.

5. Now, imagine yourself moving around and feeling more peaceful and joyful.

6. Keep breathing slowly and taking in your surroundings while experiencing them with each of your five senses.

7. Imagine positive vibes and harmony entering your body and the negative vibes leaving with every breath.

8. To finish your visualization session, slowly open your eyes and continue breathing until you are ready to move.

Breathing

Whatever you face in life, you always remind yourself to breathe. Breathing can soothe your body and mind to calm you down whenever you are stressed, anxious, or scared. Various breathing exercises can raise your vibration.

Breathing Technique

Nadi Shodhana

Nadi Shodhana is a breathing exercise referred to as alternate-nostril breathing. Practice breathing exercises like meditation and visualization by sitting comfortably in a quiet space.

Instructions:

1. Use your ring finger and thumb to block each of your nostrils.
2. Breathe in through your left nostril while blocking your right one, then block the left nostril and breathe out through the right. Reverse the process by blocking your right nostril and breathing in through the left one.
3. Repeat the process a few times and prolong the inhaling and exhaling until you feel relaxed.

Sharpen Your Psychic Skills

Protecting yourself from psychic attacks involves soul cleansing and summoning your guardian angel, which you can only do by tapping into your intuition and sharpening your skills. These skills will push you to go beyond the physical and into the spiritual world.

Listen to Your Gut

Never ignore your gut feeling because it's usually right. If someone or something makes you feel uncomfortable or even sick, this is your intuition telling you to assess the situation since something isn't right. Everyone has an inner voice, but only a few connect with and experience it. Stay attuned to this voice; when it warns you against something, take it seriously.

Use Your Five Senses

Process information and feel everything around you using your five senses. You will probably see and hear things other people don't, but you won't notice them without employing all your senses.

Be Prepared

When you sharpen your psychic skills, you begin to receive various messages. However, some will not make sense. Believe that whatever you see is real, even if it's something simple like an object or a name. You can only sharpen your skills by taking every message you receive seriously. You will experience negative energies since you are open and ready to receive anything that comes to you. Teach yourself not to pay attention to negativity by letting it flow through you or practice any techniques to raise your vibration.

Throughout your life, you will attract all energy forms. When your psychic skills are sharpened, it leaves you open to good and harmful vibes. Raising your vibration protects you against negativity. The techniques in this chapter should become a part of your daily routine to act as a weapon against the negative energies you constantly receive. Eventually, practicing these techniques becomes habitual, and your intuition and vibrations will automatically alert you to harmful energies against you, your family, and your loved ones. When you are experienced and confident using these techniques, teach them to those you deeply care about, so they can gain the same protection, positivity, and happiness as you.

Remember, positivity attracts good vibes, and negativity attracts bad ones. When you replace emotions like sadness and anger with joy and gratitude, you invite good things into your life, raising your vibration and preparing you for cleansing your karma and soul.

Chapter 3: Soul and Karma Cleansing

Like you take precautions to maintain good health, prevention techniques are the most effective way to approach psychic defense issues. This approach aims to restore balance and harmony, which can help prevent disturbances that can throw you off center. Regular spiritual cleansing practice can strengthen you to withstand psychic attacks better, leaving you less vulnerable to harm. These basic psychic care forms can help you develop psychic immunity to most forms of harm and provide protection against external negative influences.

Soul and karma cleansing can help restore your life's balance.

You've studied the concept of energy bodies in the previous chapters and are now aware of how they can affect your overall well-being. Caring for your energy body is just as important as caring for your physical hygiene. Like you prevent physical bacteria from accumulating and consuming life-giving substances for your physical body, you must do the same for your spiritual body. Your day-to-day interactions leave your energy body unbalanced and contaminated.

Although many believe they only have one body with an animating force known as the soul, true psychic individuals recognize that humans have different energy bodies making up their unique blend of energies. Metaphysicians categorize these energy bodies differently. Some systems have seven, nine, ten, or twelve bodies, each with unique attributes. However, regardless of the name or culture, these more complex systems can usually be simplified down to four bodies based on the four elements. Each body has specific needs and methods of care and cleansing, and each element offers its path to psychic hygiene on various levels.

The techniques for elemental hygiene overlap in purpose and execution since the spiritual bodies interpenetrate each other. Finding at least one technique that resonates with you and using it often is important. Each body's health is dependent on the health of the others. Changes in one body affect all the others, from the subtlest to the denser levels and back again, so you shouldn't neglect the cleansing process of any energy body. Below are in-depth explanations of how each energy body works, what role it plays, and how you can cleanse them from external energy contamination:

The Physical Body

The physical body is probably the easiest concept to grasp. It consists of flesh, blood, organs, and bones. The physical body is associated with the earth element, considered the densest of all four elements. So, the most powerful and earthy cleansing techniques are required for the spiritual cleansing of the physical body. These techniques include simple rituals with straightforward physical actions and can have a far-reaching effect on all your energy bodies. The most common cleansing ritual is smudging, a simple but powerful ritual that many people do almost daily.

Smudging is passing yourself, others, or objects through the sacred smoke of a blessed incense. The smoke is believed to purify and cleanse the person or object energetically. Although smudging is mostly used to cleanse a space or object, it can cleanse people. The materials used in smudging, like woods, herbs, and resins, are derived from the natural world, i.e., organic and in harmony with the earth element. When burned, the materials' vibration intensifies and is released into the intended space, emanating much further than the visible smoke. It is further intensified when the incense is blessed.

People refer to lower, slower, and more stagnant energies when discussing "negative" or harmful energy. Burning a powerfully protective and cleansing incense forces these lower vibrations to match or be removed from the area, as they cannot exist at that lower, dense level when surrounded by refined energy. The higher energy entrains the lower energy to match it; if it cannot, it must leave the sacred space.

Instructions for Smudging

Various incense forms are available, including wands, cones, sticks, and granules. Smudge wands are bundles of dried herbs tightly packed together. Although these can be purchased commercially, it can be fun to make them yourself. Gather fresh herbs and lay them together. Wrap them tightly with cotton string and allow them to dry evenly on a screen. Then light the tip and blow it out to create sacred smoke. Ensure you have a flameproof vessel to hold under the smudge stick, such as an earthen bowl or seashell.

Powdered incense is messier but provides a more "witchy" vibe. Grind your herbs to a powder using a traditional mortar and pestle or an electric grinder. Then, get some charcoal blocks or discs, commonly sold in stores, to use as your combustible base. Light the charcoal and sprinkle the incense on it to burn, adding more incense occasionally if you need more smoke. Use a nonflammable utensil to brush off the accumulated ash and add more herbs.

Once the incense is smoking, pass whatever objects you are clearing through the smoke. When smudging yourself, waft the smoke all over your body, including the front and back. Feathers, like turkey or crow feathers, are often used with traditional sage wands or other herb bundles to fan the embers and create more smoke.

Smudging can be ceremonial. Hold the burning incense to the north, east, south, west, above, below near the ground, left side, right side, and then the heart, asking for the blessing of all the directions and gods before smudging yourself, someone else, or an object. Being present and aware of your body is essential to truly protect the physical body. Center yourself through rituals like smudging. By being aware, you react more effectively to difficult situations.

The Emotional Body

The emotional body is known by different names, which include the astral body, psychic body, and dream body. Symbolized by the water element, it flows and takes shape like water in a vessel, with the force of imagination and willpower giving it form. When you connect with them during your sleep, your thoughts, hopes, dreams, and fears take shape on the astral plane. Similarly, your emotions take on shape and form, flow easily like water, and are susceptible to emotional pollutants and toxins from others if you lack strong boundaries.

Empathy is the ability to feel and relate to someone else's emotions and points of view. An energy can be a blessing or a curse depending on how it is expressed and handled. It is a great gift when you are solid in your personal foundation and use your sensitivity to gain greater awareness of relationships and situations. Those with healthy empathy often become healers, teachers, therapists, social workers, artists, performers, and musicians.

However, uncontrolled empathy can be overwhelming and confusing, and without strong boundaries, it is hard to discern which feelings come from an outside source and which are yours. Regular, disciplined meditation and rituals of an introspective nature, with boundary and healing techniques, are helpful for those with strong empathy issues.

Setting boundaries is key to managing empathic abilities, including shielding yourself from the emotional energy of others and recognizing when to step back and focus on your emotional well-being. Regularly practicing self-care to avoid burnout and becoming overwhelmed is important.

In addition to empathy, other forms of psychic sensitivity affect the emotional body. These include clairvoyance, clairaudience, and clairsentience, among others. Each of these abilities has a different way of perceiving psychic information and uniquely impacts the emotional body.

Developing and honing these abilities can be a valuable tool for understanding and navigating the emotional landscape of yourself and others. However, approaching these abilities with responsibility and discernment and seeking guidance and support is crucial.

Ritual Bathing

Ritual bathing is a powerful technique to cleanse and heal the emotional body. The purifying qualities of water should not be underestimated. While many witchcraft traditions emphasize the importance of a ritual bath before serious workings, most witches skip the bath and jump straight into spells. However, when engaging in a ritual bath, the ritual has a more charged, more psychic, and more magnetic quality. Water has the ability to cleanse the emotional and physical body, and using protective and cleansing herbs in ritual baths infuses the water with their properties. Salts draw out dense energies, and vinegar neutralizes harmful energies. For example, vinegar can be left in a bowl to absorb and collect harmful energies and then discarded into the earth or down a drain.

Here is a cleansing bath salt recipe with a mix of sea salt, lavender flowers or leaves, yarrow flowers or leaves, mugwort or myrrh, and lavender and myrrh essential oil.

1. Mix the ingredients together while holding each one (except for the oils) in your hands, allowing your energy to mingle with the natural healing powers of each ingredient.

2. When the ingredients are mixed, place the mixture in an airtight bottle for a few weeks to allow the scents to mingle.

3. Place a few tablespoons of the mixture in a muslin or cotton bag and submerge it in the bath water.

4. When ready to get out of the bath, allow the water to drain while sitting in the tub. It allows unwanted energies to go down the drain and be neutralized with salt and herbs.

Floral Rituals

Another water-based protection method is using herbal and floral waters - rose water is the most common and powerful. Rose water can be bought at drug stores or made at home using rose essential oil, water, and alcohol. The number of essential oil drops varies depending on the preferred strength of the scent. Another method for making rose water is making a tea infusion of rose petals and water, then mixing it with the water and alcohol solution. A true hydrosol can be created using a large pot, two smaller bowls, and a cover with rose petals and water. The water collected in the bowl is your rose water, known as rose hydrosol, which should be preserved with alcohol or glycerin.

Roses are spiritually uplifting and grounding and are considered the vibration of pure love. They are the most protective substance in many traditions. The flower symbolizes love, while the thorns symbolize protection. If rose water or oil is unavailable, you can visualize roses around you for protection, inviting the rose flower's spirit, which wilts in the mind's eye as it absorbs harmful energy.

The Mental Body

The mind is the body, often requiring the most cleansing. Typically, the mind is chaotic and cluttered, making it difficult to find and utilize useful information without being hindered by accumulated waste from the past. Consequently, the spiritual process is primarily about eliminating excess baggage from your mental closet to establish harmony and order. While generating millions of thoughts daily, the majority are repeated, following familiar, static patterns and rarely creating anything new. Thoughts are less dense and create feelings, while emotions are denser than thoughts. Focusing on a thought long enough can conjure up associated feelings creating sensations and bodily reactions measurable in the physical world. The physical world is denser than the emotional world. Therefore, the state of mind determines health at the emotional and physical levels.

True innovators and magical individuals can think beyond the usual patterns and habits to see things differently. The mental bodies must be trained similarly to physical bodies. Traditional school work, like math and memorization, is helpful but not the most powerful technique, as it can trap the mind into patterns. Mental cleansing is not about thinking like everyone else but about discovering your true self. The most mentally cleansing experiences are those eliminating what does not serve the mind and helping train the mind to be a tool, servant, and aid instead of the master. Mental introspection is the key, which brings awareness to the habits and patterns contributing to undesirable events in your life.

Journaling is an excellent starting point for introspective work. Writing down the things in your mind establishes discipline and enables you to identify patterns consciously. Keeping a dream journal to help reflect on the subconscious themes manifested in sleep is essential.

Regular meditation is another tool for mental hygiene. It involves taking time to be quiet and listen to your highest guidance. Various meditation techniques are available, such as Eastern techniques of watching the mind, focusing on the breath, or using a mantra, and Western visualization and relaxation techniques. Regular meditation reduces stress, increases vitality, and enhances creativity.

The Soul Body

The soul body is connected to the fire element, representing the personal spark of divinity within everyone. The soul is often referred to as the higher self and is associated with the highest level of spiritual knowledge. It is the most energetic and elusive part of yourself and, therefore, the most protected and untouchable from external harm. The fiery nature of the soul prevents the accumulation of harmful energy, burning away that which doesn't serve you in a positive way. You achieve true protection, fearlessness, and eternal wisdom by identifying with the soul rather than the mind, emotions, or body. In true essence, you are connected to all things yet bound by none.

The techniques for healing and protection use fire to extend divine energy from the soul into other subtle bodies. The first technique is getting in touch with solar fire directly by going outside into the sunlight for five to ten minutes daily. It allows the Sun's spiritual energy to burn harmful energies that could have accumulated and fill your aura with vital life energy, making you healthier and more resistant to harm. The second technique is visualizing the Sun while in meditation and drawing down the Sun's golden white light to surround and revitalize you.

You must think of yourself as existing on all four spiritual levels simultaneously and seek balance and harmony with your physical, emotional, mental, and soul components to achieve true health. Mastery of these levels provides spiritual protection, so you don't have to be in a deep trance or perform an in-depth ritual to invite the healing energies of fire, light, and the Sun for health and protection.

Understanding Karma

The concept of karma is not complex or abstract. It refers to your actions and the consequences that arise from them. Karma is a cycle of cause and effect that shapes lives. Your past actions influence your present and future experiences. Positive actions create love-based karma, which brings valuable lessons for personal growth. In contrast, negative actions create fear-based karma, often leading to judgment and consequences. However, negative karma can be transformed into positive by showing love, compassion, and forgiveness to yourself and others.

Maintaining purity in thoughts, words, and actions is essential to create good karma. Despite your best intentions, sometimes you cause pain or hurt. In these situations, acknowledging your mistakes, learning from them, and making amends is crucial. Forgiving yourself and others to prevent negative energy from returning is vital.

You must send love and light to everyone, avoid hidden motives or control dramas, cultivate gratitude, and practice forgiveness to create positive karma. Forgiveness is a challenging but essential practice to manifest love-based karma. Guilt and negative emotions can lead to unnecessary suffering, but you can move forward and grow by forgiving yourself and others. Remember, mistakes are part of being human, and you can always learn from them.

Further Techniques for Cleansing the Soul

- **Sound healing:** Sound healing uses sound frequencies to balance the mind, body, and soul. It uses instruments like singing bowls, gongs, or tuning forks to produce vibrations penetrating the body and help release blocked energy. You can attend a sound healing session with a practitioner or perform it at home by playing soothing music and focusing on the vibrations.

- **Chakra cleansing:** Chakras are energy centers in the body that can become blocked or imbalanced, leading to physical and emotional issues. Chakra cleansing uses various techniques to release blockages and balance the energy flow. Techniques can include visualization, meditation, or crystals.

- **Breathwork:** Breathwork uses specific breathing techniques to access different states of consciousness and release stored emotions or trauma. It can be done with a practitioner or at home using guided breathwork meditations.

- **Forest Bathing:** Forest Bathing, known as *shinrin-yoku*, is a Japanese practice of immersing yourself in nature and using all your senses to connect with the environment. It can help reduce stress and anxiety, boost mood, and promote calm and relaxation.

- **Cord Cutting:** Cord cutting is a visualization technique of cutting energetic cords between yourself and another person or situation. It can help you to release negative energy, let go of past traumas, and create healthy boundaries.

• **Shamanic Journeying:** Shamanic journeying uses rhythmic drumming or other sounds to enter into an altered state of consciousness. During this state, you can connect with your inner wisdom, spirit guides, and other sources of guidance and healing.

Soul and karma cleansing are vital practices for anyone seeking a balanced and fulfilling life. Your actions, thoughts, and emotions create your karma, affecting you and those around you. Purifying your soul and clearing karmic debts aligns you with a higher purpose and living in harmony with the universe. It is not always an easy journey, and setbacks will occur, but with dedication, patience, and perseverance, you can transform and positively impact the world. Remember, the power to cleanse your soul and karma lies within you. It is never too late to start. So, take the first step today, and begin your journey toward a brighter future.

Chapter 4: Cleansing Your Space and Others

Past energies and influences attach themselves to people and places. For instance, if you fought with your spouse in your living room, the space would be filled with negativity that won't disappear until you perform a cleansing ritual. For this reason, people usually purify their homes after a divorce, bad breakup, or financial trouble to remove the impact of these negative experiences. Cleansing an area is similar to pressing a reset button, turning it back to its original high frequency before negative energy impacts its vibration.

Cleansing your space will clear the negative energy surrounding it.
https://www.pexels.com/photo/a-woman-holding-a-sage-with-smoke-6628539/

Cleansing your home is necessary before performing spiritual or energy work. Even if you haven't experienced negativity, you should still cleanse the place at least once a week because you never know what negative vibes your or your family members have brought in recently. Clearing negative energy frees space for positive vibes to enter your home and life.

It is similar to getting the flu. After you recover, you usually wash your linens and clothes and take a shower to wash away the germs. You open the windows to clear your home from sickly vibes and allow energy to flow. Afterward, you feel lighter and better. The same happens when you cleanse a room. You will feel the space's vibe changing, impacting your mood.

Since people and objects vibrate in different frequencies, lower vibes usually rise slightly to meet higher frequencies. However, high vibration drops so the two can meet in the middle. For instance, bringing a crystal to your unclean space will raise the area's frequency, but the crystal's vibe will lower to match the surrounding energy.

Keep your space protected by constantly performing purification rituals, especially after you have guests, to clear the impact of their energy. Regular cleansing makes it easier to eliminate unwanted vibrations before they cause serious damage.

If you want to raise protection around a specific space, ensure it is free of lingering negative energy. You can tell a room has low vibration from the moment you enter because you will feel uncomfortable or tense immediately. Check the place's energy before you begin working, even if you have recently cleansed it. Your spouse or a family member could have had an argument at home and lowered its vibe.

Negative Energy in Your Home

You are probably wondering if your home has negative energy or not. Often, you can sense these vibes in the room, but if you are stressed or anxious, it can be hard to separate your negative emotions from the house's vibes. However, there are certain signs to look out for indicating negative energy in your home is affecting you and your family.

Bad Relationships

Look at the relationship of everyone in the house. Are you constantly arguing with your spouse? Are your children always fighting with one another? Do you feel your relationship with your family is strained? It could result in negative vibes in your home.

Constant Complaining

There is no denying that life is stressful, and you can catch yourself occasionally complaining about your work, your terrible boss, or the traffic. However, if you and your family constantly complain – even when things are going well – and you can't find the good in life, your home requires cleansing.

Excessive Blame

If everyone in your home is always blaming and criticizing each other and refusing to take responsibility for their actions, this could be the impact of negative vibes.

Clutter

Clutter doesn't only lower your vibes, but it also spreads negative energy around your home. Crowded furniture and mess can create a chaotic environment. Your furniture should be arranged so it allows energy to flow easily around the house,

Cleansing a space is very simple. You can do many weekly or daily rituals that won't take much time or effort.

This chapter covers various rituals to purify your home, altar, or other spaces.

Declutter and Clean Your Home

Remove all the items you don't need and vacuum and dust every corner of your home. Don't keep broken items like a cracked vase because they invite negative vibes. After decluttering, cleanse the house with this purifying solution you can easily make at home.

Ingredients:

- 1 cup of sea salt
- 5 lemons
- ¼ cup of white vinegar

Instructions:

1. Fill a bucket with water, add the sea salt and white vinegar, then squeeze in the lemons.
2. Using a towel, clean the window, frames, doors, and doorknobs.

Build an Altar

Altars are the perfect place for spiritual work but can also release negative energy or invite positive energy.

Instructions:

1. Set the altar in the space where you will perform your spiritual work.

2. Set an intention for the altar, like inviting positive energy into your home.

3. Clean the area by removing the dust and decluttering the space.

4. Place various objects symbolizing protection, abundance, good health, good fortune, and prosperity. In other words, add objects representing the energy you want in your home.

5. Add crystals, flowers, pictures, statues, candles, incense, or other objects that bring you comfort and happiness.

6. Organize all the items on your altar and avoid cluttering it or the space around it.

Smudge Ritual #1

Burning herbs is one of the oldest cleansing rituals. The Native Americans used it for centuries to cleanse themselves and their homes of negative energy. This ritual's recipe includes multiple dried herbs, but you can use only a couple if you prefer.

Ingredients:

- Basil
- Pine cones
- Cloves
- Lavender
- Rosemary
- Juniper
- Sweetgrass
- Cedar
- Palo santo
- Garden sage

• White sage

Instructions:

1. Open the house windows to allow the negative energy to escape.

2. Set an intention of what you hope to achieve from this ritual, like cleansing your home of negative vibes, or think of mantras and affirmations, like *"I am cleansing this room of negative energy to free space for love and light."*

3. Wrap the herbs in a bundle and light them at one end until they release smoke.

4. Gently fan the smoke with your hand, then move clockwise around the room to cleanse the desired space while repeating the intention.

Smudge Ritual #2

Ingredients and Tools:

• Sage with dragon blood or white sage

• A candle

• Incense (choose your favorite scent)

• A ceramic dish for the incense

• Sweetgrass essential oil

Instructions:

1. Organize and declutter the space before you begin the ritual, then open the windows.

2. Burn the sage and move clockwise around the room while thinking about the positive vibes you want to surround yourself with and what you plan to do with the cleansed space.

3. Put the sage on a dish, place it in the center of your home, and leave it to burn.

4. Now you have released the negative energy and freed space to welcome positive vibes.

5. Sweetgrass can attract positive energy, so apply 10 to 20 drops of sweetgrass essential oil in a diffuser. It is more effective to use it directly after the sage.

Spray Ritual

Ingredients and Tools:

- Essential oils (use any oils you prefer)
- Pure alcohol
- Distilled water
- Spray bottle (glass or plastic)

Instructions:

1. Pour 50 ml of water into an empty glass, then add 20 drops of essential oils.
2. Mix the alcohol with the water.
3. Pour the mixture into a diffuser or a spray bottle, then spray the room you wish to cleanse while repeating your intention.

Burn Ritual

Tools:

- Paper
- Pen
- Candle
- Crystal
- Cinnamon stick

Instructions:

1. Write down what you hope to achieve from this cleansing ritual on the piece of paper, fold it, and place it in front of you.
2. Light the candle and use it to light your cinnamon stick.
3. Place the cinnamon stick and the crystal on the area you want to cleanse and leave them for a few minutes (keep your eyes on the cinnamon stick because it can be a fire hazard).
4. Burn the piece of paper in the candle.

Salt Ritual

In some cultures, salt symbolizes purity and can cleanse an area of negative energy and raise its vibes.

Ingredients:

• Salt

Instructions:

1. Pour a small amount of salt into a bowl and place it at your front door to prevent negative energy from entering your home.

2. Remove the objects from the area you want to cleanse, dust the corners, and sprinkle salt around the room.

3. Ensure the salt remains undisturbed for a couple of days, so keep children and pets away from the room.

Tuning Fork Ritual

Ancient cultures used the power of sound and music to heal different ailments. In ancient Greece, physicians used singing bowls, instruments, and vibrations as sound therapy to treat insomnia. Certain sound frequencies can clear the air from negative energy caused by stress and tension.

Tools:

• Tuning fork

Instructions:

1. Sit in a comfortable position.

2. Set an intention for cleansing your area and renewing the energy.

3. Gently tap the tuning fork against a table or solid space.

4. Close your eyes and feel the sound vibrating in every area around the room.

5. Repeat the process until you feel the vibes in the room rising.

Bell Ritual

Since sound can be an effective weapon against negative energy, you can use other methods like ringing a bell. Ring a bell in different rooms around your home, and the vibration will spread across the house, releasing negative energy.

Visualization Ritual

Instructions:

1. Sit in a quiet room without distractions and relax your body and mind.
2. Close your eyes and take deep and slow breaths.
3. Imagine a ball of golden light floating next to your heart.
4. The light keeps expanding with every breath until it exits your body.
5. Spread the light around the area you wish to cleanse while setting an intention.
6. When you have finished, slowly open your eyes and express your gratitude.

Lemon Ritual

Have you ever wondered why many cleaning products contain lemon as their main ingredient? Lemon's scent is uplifting and can alter the energy of the room.

Tips:

- Put 20 drops of lemon essential oil in a diffuser and place it in the room you want to cleanse.
- Cut lemons into slices and put them in a few bowls in different corners around the house.
- Simmer lemon peels and let the steam fill the house.

Water Ritual

Ingredients:

- Water
- Orange blossom water, rose water, or your favorite essential oil

Instructions:

1. Pour filtered water into a bucket and add 2 to 5 drops of essential oil, rose water, or orange blossom water.
2. Add cleaning soap to the bucket and cleanse your floors, windows, and front door.

Reiki Ritual

You don't need a practitioner for this ritual; you can do it yourself at home.

Instructions:

1. Sit in a comfortable position and close your eyes.

2. Breathe deeply and focus on your breath.

3. Visualize healing white light flowing into you from your head, then into your body, and exiting through your hands.

4. Feel the healing power inside you, filling you with loving and positive energy.

5. Release this healing energy through your hands into the room

6. When you finish, express your gratitude for the healing energy.

Crystals Ritual

Tools:

- Smoky quartz
- Onyx
- Black tourmaline

Instructions:

1. Place these crystals in the room or space you wish to cleanse and leave them for a few days.

2. Afterward, cleanse the crystals from the negative energy by leaving them overnight under the moonlight.

Open Windows

Fresh air can clear negative energy from your home and replace it with positive vibes. Open all your windows and allow the fresh air to fill the place. You can turn on the fans to allow air circulation and open your drawers and closets to release stagnant energy.

Repaint Your Walls

Look at your house's walls. If the colors are dark or dull and make you feel stressed or down, it is time for some interior design. Repaint the walls with a bright color or apply an interesting wallpaper. You can add wall art and other decoration to liven the place and release negative vibes.

Cleansing Your Children

You love no one more than your child and want to protect them from harm. It is hard for a parent to believe their kid is exposed to negative energy. However, children can experience stress, anxiety, and toxic vibes daily. Although you can't shield them from the world, you can prevent the negativity from ruining their lives. Certain techniques can cleanse your little one from negative energy.

Visualization

You have learned that visualization is a powerful technique against negative energy. Similar to using this method to raise your vibe and purify your home, you can use it to cleanse your child from negative energy. However, they cannot do this technique themselves, so you must do it for them.

Instructions:

1. Sit in a quiet room in a comfortable position and close your eyes.

2. Visualize white protective light wrapping your child.

3. Spend a few minutes focusing on this image, slowly open your eyes, and express your gratitude.

Spinal Flush

Perform this technique on your child after they have been exposed to negative situations or people.

Instructions:

1. Place your hand on the top of your child's spine between the shoulders and neck.

2. Slowly and gently move your hand down to their tailbone, then up again.

3. Tell your child to take deep breaths while you move your hand.

4. Repeat this motion six times.

Now, teach your child how to protect their energy or "zip it up."

1. Place your hand at the center of your child's front torso.

2. Pretend they are wearing a vest with a zipper that goes up to their chin.

3. Using your hand, pretend you are zipping up the indivisible vest from the bottom to the top.

4. Repeat the motions four times.

Teach your child to do the "zip up" motion. It is a simple and fun exercise they will enjoy doing throughout the day to contain their energy.

Tiny Coal Cure

This method works for a baby or a toddler. Negative energy can impact newborns. If you had guests recently, their negative vibes could rub off on your baby, causing irritability, constant crying, and sickness. Coal cure is an effective treatment to protect your baby against negative energy.

Ingredients and Tools:

- Cold water with 5 ice cubes
- 9 classic matches
- A tall glass

Instructions:

1. Set your intentions and repeat them in a low voice or merely think of them. Don't say them out loud; you should be quiet for this method to work.

2. Pour the water and ice cubes into the tall glass.

3. Light each match above the glass of water and focus on the flame.

4. When half the match is burned, drop it into the water.

5. Count each match and add "not" before the number, like not one, not two, not three, etc.

6. If the matches remain above the water, your child isn't affected by negative energy. If the matches fall to the bottom of the glass, your child has been exposed to bad vibes.

7. Say a little prayer or affirmation to bless the water and use the cure to heal your child from negative energy.

8. Place your fingers in the water and run them across your child's forehead.

9. Dip your fingers and gently rub the sides of their eyes and temples.

10. Dip your fingers in the water and rub their neck to wash away the negativity.

11. Again, dip your fingers and rub their left arm beginning at the shoulder until you reach their fingers. Pretend you are pulling the energy from their body.

12. Repeat the previous step on their right leg.

13. Dip your fingers and move your hand from their belly to their foot.

14. Dip your fingers again and move them down along each leg and pretend you are pulling negative vibes away from them.

15. Pour the remaining water outside your home.

16. You can practice this ritual on children of any age or a loved one, like your parents or spouse.

Protecting Your Pets

Your fur children deserve protection, too. Negative energy can affect pets, especially if your home has bad vibes. Animals are more susceptible to negativity than people since they are more in sync with the universe. These methods can cleanse them from negative energy and keep them protected.

Practice Reiki

Take your pet to a reiki practitioner, or you can do it yourself using the reiki ritual mentioned previously.

Use Crystals

Hang healing crystals on their collar, under their bed, or in water. However, be careful since only a few crystals are safe to put in water, like clear quartz, smokey quartz, or rose quartz. Don't add small stones; your pet will swallow them, so opt for big ones.

Place Spiritual symbols on Your Pet

Place a spiritual symbol on your pet's collar, like the evil eye, OM symbol, or Hamsa Hand, to protect them against negative energy.

Visualization

Employ the same visualization technique you used on your child to cleanse your pet.

You can protect your house, children, pets, and loved ones from the impact of negative energy. The rituals do not have to be complicated and complex to cleanse your home. Regularly repeat these simple and easy rituals to keep your home and family safe.

Chapter 5: Post-Cleanse: Healing Your Aura

You've learned to cleanse your psychic energy and the spaces around you from negative contamination. As you work through the techniques, you'll notice an incredible lightness and clarity within your soul as you shed layers of negativity. However, there's yet another aspect to consider: your aura. Imagine your soul as a freshly cleaned and polished mirror reflecting the purest version of yourself. It reflects your state when you have cleansed and purified your psychic energy.

Auras are energy fields that surround the physical body.

But, when you step back into the world, you soon realize the mirror is not as pure as you thought. It's surrounded by a haze of dust, scratches, and smudges. The same is the case for your aura. Even though you've cleansed your energy, your aura can still be contaminated by the negative energy and experiences you've gone through. Each speck of dust and scratch on the surface represents an emotion, experience, or thought that has impacted you. These imprints can distort the reflection of your soul and make it harder to connect with your true self.

The concept of an aura is often dismissed as pseudoscience, but it has been present in various cultures throughout history. The aura can be defined as a subtle energy field surrounding and permeating the physical body, containing information about your physical, emotional, and spiritual state. It is connected to the soul and affected by thoughts, emotions, and experiences. While intangible, it can profoundly impact your well-being and ability to navigate the world around you.

Your aura is a protective shield around you, absorbing and filtering energies from your surroundings. Like any shield, it's prone to wear down over time, leaving you vulnerable to harmful attacks. If your aura is not energized and cleansed, negative energies can seep through the cracks in your protective shield and weaken your aura, making you more susceptible to harm. This damaged aura can manifest as physical, emotional, and mental imbalances if left unchecked. Consequently, giving your aura the attention and care it requires is imperative.

When you cleanse, heal, and strengthen your aura, you ultimately enhance your ability to navigate the world and connect better with your psychic self. But the question is, where do you start? This chapter provides a complete guide to cleansing and healing your aura from the damage inflicted upon it. You can use several techniques, like smudging, crystal healing, or salt baths. You'll learn to restore your aura's balance, remove remnant negative energies, and revitalize your psychic aura. Furthermore, you'll understand the relationship between a healed aura and psychic protection and how a strong aura can enhance your spiritual growth.

What Is an Aura?

An aura is a subtle energy field surrounding and permeating the physical body. It is often described as a luminous field of color seen or felt by sensitive individuals. The aura's purpose is multi-faceted and has been studied by various spiritual traditions and energy healers. One of the aura's primary functions is to protect the physical body from external negative energies. The aura acts as a shield absorbing and filtering out negative energies before they can enter the body. Therefore, many energy healers recommend people take measures to protect their aura, such as wearing protective crystals, practicing meditation, or avoiding negative people or environments.

Another function of the aura is to reflect the state of the body, mind, and soul. The aura's colors, textures, and patterns can change depending on a person's emotional state, physical health, and spiritual well-being. Energy healers use this information to diagnose and treat imbalances within a person's energy field. The aura is also a conduit for spiritual energy and communication. The aura is connected to the spiritual realms and can act as a bridge between the physical world and the higher planes of existence. Through practices like meditation, prayer, or energy healing, individuals can open and activate their aura to receive divine guidance, healing, and inspiration.

How an Aura Is Connected to the Soul

The soul is often described as the essence of a person. It is the part that transcends the physical body and exists beyond the limits of time and space. In contrast, the aura is the energetic counterpart of the physical body and is closely connected to the soul. The aura is an extension of the soul, reflecting its qualities and characteristics. The colors and patterns of the aura can reveal aspects of a person's spiritual nature, including their level of consciousness, inner strengths and weaknesses, and connection to the divine.

The aura is intimately connected to the chakra system, a series of energy centers along the spine. Each chakra corresponds to a different aspect of the body, mind, and soul and influences the aura's qualities associated with that area. For example, the heart chakra is associated with love, compassion, and connection to others and influences the color and texture of the aura in that area. The crown chakra is associated with spiritual connection, enlightenment, and transcendence and influences the higher layers of the aura.

The Different Layers of the Aura

The aura is often described as having multiple layers with unique characteristics and functions. While different traditions and energy healers use slightly different terminology or descriptions for these layers, there are generally considered the aura's seven main layers.

1. **The Physical Layer:** This layer is closest to the physical body and is primarily associated with physical sensations. It is seen as a band of light surrounding the body, extending about one inch to several feet beyond the skin.

2. **The Emotional Layer:** This layer is associated with emotions and feelings and can be seen as a cloud of color surrounding the body. Depending on a person's emotional state, the layer's colors can change rapidly.

3. **The Mental Layer:** This layer is associated with thoughts, ideas, and beliefs and is seen as a network of lines or patterns of light surrounding the body.

4. **The Astral Layer:** This layer is associated with the astral or spiritual realm and is seen as a mist or fog surrounding the body. It is the bridge between the physical and spiritual realms and often the focus of astral projection or out-of-body experiences.

5. **The Etheric Layer:** This layer is associated with vitality and life force energy and is seen as a web or matrix of light surrounding the body. It is often described as the blueprint for the physical body and influences a person's physical health and well-being.

6. **The Celestial Layer:** This layer is associated with higher consciousness and spiritual connection and is seen as a bright, shimmering light surrounding the body. It is often described as the gateway to the divine and is the focus of many spiritual practices and meditations.

7. **The Ketheric Layer:** This layer is associated with the highest levels of consciousness and spiritual enlightenment and is seen as a brilliant, golden light surrounding the body. It is the source of all spiritual energy and the ultimate goal of many spiritual practices and paths.

Each layer of the aura has unique qualities and functions. However, they are all interconnected and influence one another. Individuals can enhance their spiritual growth and connect more deeply with their innermost selves and the divine by purifying and activating each aural layer.

What Can Damage Your Aura?

The aura is a subtle energy field constantly interacting with the environment and is influenced by numerous factors. While the aura is designed to protect the physical body from external negative energies, several things can damage or weaken the aura, including negative emotions and experiences, exposure to harmful energies, and lack of self-care.

1. Negative Emotions and Experiences

Negative emotions and experiences significantly impact the aura. When a person experiences strong emotions, like fear, anger, or sadness, the aura can become clouded or discolored, reflecting the negative energy generated. Over time, repeated exposure to negative emotions can cause the aura to become weakened or damaged, making it more vulnerable to external negative energies. In addition to negative emotions, negative experiences, such as trauma or abuse, can profoundly affect the aura. Traumatic experiences can leave energetic imprints on the aura, causing persistent emotional and physical symptoms. These imprints can be difficult to clear and could require assistance from an energy healer or therapist.

2. Exposure to Harmful Energies

Exposure to harmful energies can damage the aura. Harmful energies can come from a variety of sources, including electromagnetic radiation from electronic devices, geopathic stress from underground water veins or fault lines, and negative energies from people or environments. Electromagnetic radiation from electronic devices, such as computers, cell phones, and televisions, can disrupt the aura's energy field, causing it to weaken or become imbalanced. Geopathic stress, caused by natural radiation from the earth, can negatively affect the aura.

Negative energies from people or environments can harm the aura. Being around negative people or in negative environments can cause the aura to become clouded or discolored, reflecting the negative energy. Being mindful of the people and environments surrounding you and taking steps to protect your aura is important.

3. Lack of Self-Care

A lack of self-care can also damage the aura. Neglecting your physical, emotional, and spiritual needs can cause the aura to become weakened or imbalanced. This includes not getting enough sleep, not eating a healthy diet, not engaging in regular exercise, or not practicing self-care activities, like meditation or yoga. Neglecting your emotional and spiritual needs can negatively affect the aura. Therefore, addressing emotional or spiritual imbalances you might be experiencing and taking steps to heal and strengthen the energy field is essential. Healing methods can include working with an energy healer or a therapist, engaging in spiritual practices like meditation or prayer, or cultivating positive relationships and environments.

How Do You Know if Your Aura Needs Healing?

The aura is a constantly evolving energy field that can weaken or become damaged over time. Awareness of the signs and symptoms of a damaged aura and cultivating self-awareness and intuition to know when your aura needs healing are vital. Various methods, like energy readings and aura photography, are available to provide additional insight into your aura's state.

Signs and Symptoms of a Damaged Aura

Several signs and symptoms can indicate your aura is damaged or needs healing. These include:

- Feeling emotionally drained or overwhelmed
- Experiencing physical symptoms such as fatigue, headaches, or digestive issues
- Feeling disconnected from your body or surroundings
- Being overly sensitive to other people's emotions or energy
- Feeling anxious, depressed, or moody
- Having difficulty sleeping or experiencing vivid dreams
- Feeling heaviness or pressure around the head or shoulders
- Experiencing being spiritually blocked or stuck

Other factors, like physical illness or stress, could cause these symptoms. However, suppose you experience persistent or unexplained symptoms. In that case, it is worth exploring if your aura contributes to your overall health and well-being.

Self-Awareness and Intuition

Self-awareness and intuition are important tools for assessing your aura's state. You can become more attuned to your energy field and better identify when something feels "off" by practicing self-reflection and mindfulness. Paying attention to your intuition and listening to your inner voice provides valuable insight into your aura's condition and whether it requires healing.

Energy Readings and Aura Photography

Energy readings and aura photography are useful tools for those interested in more objective methods of assessing their aura. Energy readings require working with an energy healer or practitioner to assess your aura using various techniques, like scanning, chakra assessment, or muscle testing. Aura photography uses specialized cameras to capture images of the aura and provide visual insight into the state of your energy field.

Ways to Heal a Damaged Aura

If you have identified that your aura could be damaged or needs healing, several methods are available to help restore balance and vitality to your energy field. These methods include aura-cleansing techniques, energy-healing modalities, lifestyle changes, and self-care practices.

Aura Cleansing Techniques

Aura cleansing techniques remove negative energy and blockages from the aura, allowing it to function optimally. Some popular aura-cleansing techniques include:

- **Smudging:** Smudging involves burning herbs like sage or palo santo to clear negative energy from the aura and physical space.

- **Salt baths:** Soaking in a bath infused with Epsom salts or Himalayan salt can help draw out negative energy and promote relaxation.

- **Crystal healing:** Certain crystals, like clear quartz or amethyst, can absorb negative energy and promote healing in the aura.

- **Reiki:** Reiki is energy healing, where the practitioner channels healing energy into the recipient to balance and clear the aura.

- **Sound healing:** Sound healing uses specific frequencies and vibrations, like singing bowls or tuning forks, to promote aura healing.
- **Herbal Baths:** Soaking in a bath infused with herbs like lavender or chamomile can promote relaxation and release negative energy from the aura. Different herbs have different properties that can specifically affect the aura.
- **Flower Essences:** Flower essences are dilutions of flower extracts with energetic properties affecting the aura. These essences can be taken orally or applied topically to promote healing and balance in the aura.

Energy Healing Modalities

Energy healing modalities promote healing and balance in the body's energy systems, including the aura. Some popular energy healing modalities include:

- **Acupuncture:** Acupuncture is inserting thin needles into specific points on the body to promote balance and healing in the energy field.
- **Reflexology:** Reflexology is the application of pressure to specific points on the feet, hands, and ears to promote healing and balance in the energy field.
- **Chakra healing:** Chakra healing works with the body's energy centers (chakras) to promote balance and healing in the aura.
- **Qigong:** Qigong is a Chinese practice using slow, gentle movements, breathing techniques, and meditation to promote balance and healing in the energy field.
- **Pranic Healing:** Pranic healing uses the body's energy centers to remove blockages and promote balance and healing in the energy field.
- **Polarity Therapy:** Polarity therapy balances the body's energy field through touch, movement, and communication techniques. This modality is based on the idea that thoughts, emotions, and physical experiences affect the body's energy field.
- **Access Consciousness:** This method uses various tools and techniques, including verbal processes, bodywork, and energetic clearing, to help individuals access their inner wisdom and create

positive life changes. Among the most well-known tools are "The Bars," which touch specific points on the head to release energy blockages and promote relaxation.

Lifestyle Changes and Self-Care Practices

Lifestyle changes and self-care practices are making conscious choices to support the health and well-being of your energy field. Some of the most effective practices include:

- **Meditation:** Meditation is sitting quietly and focusing on your breath or a specific object to promote relaxation and balance in the energy field. Regular meditation can help reduce stress and promote overall well-being.

- **Exercise:** Exercise is an important part of maintaining a healthy energy field. Physical activity can help reduce stress, increase circulation, and promote overall well-being.

- **Healthy diet:** Eating a balanced and nutritious diet can help support your energy field's health by providing essential nutrients and promoting overall well-being.

- **Positive affirmations:** Positive affirmations are repeating positive statements to yourself to promote positive self-talk and emotional well-being.

- **Setting boundaries:** Setting boundaries is establishing clear limits with yourself and others to protect your energy and promote well-being.

Maintaining a Strong Aura

Maintaining a strong aura is essential for overall health and well-being. As you care for your physical body through exercise, healthy eating, and rest, you must care for your energy field to promote optimal health. Here are some creative and effective ways to keep your aura strong and vibrant:

- **Shielding:** Shielding is visualizing a protective shield around your energy field to keep negative energy out and protect your aura. You can imagine the shield as a bubble or a force field surrounding and protecting your energy field.

- **Grounding:** Grounding is connecting with the earth to promote balance and stability in your energy field. Visualize roots growing from your feet into the earth or spend time in nature, like walking barefoot on the ground.

- **Visualizations**: Visualizations use your imagination to create a positive, protective image in your mind. For example, visualize yourself surrounded by a white light protecting your energy field or surrounded by a group of supportive, positive people.

- **Color therapy**: Color therapy uses specific colors to promote balance and healing in the energy field. For example, wearing or surrounding yourself with the color green can promote balance and harmony, while blue can promote calm and communication.

- **Feng shui**: Creating a harmonious and balanced living space through feng shui can help promote a strong aura. It involves arranging your space to promote good energy flow and balance.

By incorporating these effective techniques into your daily routine, you can maintain a strong and healthy aura to support your physical, emotional, and spiritual well-being.

Various methods for healing and maintaining your aura have been provided. Many more are available from online sources or in health stores.

Healing your aura is an essential part of maintaining overall well-being and strengthening psychic protection. By understanding what an aura is, what can damage it, and how to heal it, you can control your energetic state and enhance your spiritual growth. Incorporating regular aura maintenance practices and protection techniques can help you maintain a strong aura and navigate the world with greater ease and confidence.

Chapter 6: Calling Upon Angels for Protection

Angelic beings have assisted humans for thousands of years and are more than willing to guide and help when facing an obstacle or difficult situation. This chapter explains how angels or archangels can protect you, your space, and your loved ones against psychic attacks. You'll learn that angels are beings blessed with immense powers. They can be summoned to work on your behalf, guide you through life, and envelop you with protective energies. They are spiritual creatures in many forms. However, they aren't bound to a physical presence, so they won't appear in their natural form. Angels have different purposes and jurisdictions. For example, archangels have the specialty they govern and can be summoned to resolve specific issues. They are leaders among angels and have an immense energy signature. While people are generally more sensitive to their guardian angel's energy, you can feel an energy shift in the room when an archangel appears. Guardian angels guide you through life from birth, pointing out paths and purposes and helping you heal from past traumas. They rush in to help when you need help or direct your messages to your guardian or archangels.

Guardian angels guide you throughout your life.

Guardian angels are responsible for your spiritual growth and protect you on your life's journey. Unlike archangels, which work with everyone, guardians work exclusively with their charge. Your guardian angel has a unique bond with you and provides unconditional love and support - and everything else you may need to raise your psychic defenses. While they won't interfere with your conscious decisions, they can be called upon, which is great if you need an urgent power boost to ward off negative vibes.

You can call on an angel when you struggle to keep out negative energies or fear incoming psychic attacks. However, your guardian angel is the closest to you and can absorb your emotions and vibes, so they will know you need them before you actually do. You'll feel your guardian's presence in times of despair or stress caused by negative spiritual influences. They may send you a subtle message to get your attention and help you embrace their protective powers.

Guardian angels aren't only for challenging times. You can call on them whenever you need support and psychic protection. They can help you sustain your energy and guard you as you step into uncharted territories, like meeting people you don't know (hence you are unaware of their intentions and emotions).

While angels (particularly your guardians) are keen to accept your invitation into your life, connecting with them is a highly personal process. You can invoke them as you wish. You can summon one angel or more, as sometimes psychic protection requires several layers of angelic powers.

Calling on Angels for Protection

A simple and sincere prayer is the easiest way to call on an angel. For example, you can say.

"Thank you, (the angel's name you want to summon), for guiding me through this situation. I welcome your guidance and protection."

When summoning an angel for protection, remember their spirit guides you with the highest truth. They carry incredibly high vibrations, regardless of which angel you summon. They deserve your gratitude, so it's always a great idea to begin by addressing them with a "thank you." It also reminds you that angelic help is already on its way.

When first contacting your guardian, spirit guide, or another angel, you must first introduce yourself. While they might know who you are spiritually, it doesn't hurt to be polite and respectful. Summon your guardian angel through a simple mediation.

Instructions:

1. Get comfortable in a secluded space, close your eyes, and take a few long, deep breaths.

2. Using your mind, call on your guardian angel, welcome them, and ask them to reveal their name to you.

3. Use your preferred relaxation method. Use whatever technique helps you become centered, grounded, and focused on a specific intention.

4. You can meditate for as long as you like. You may hear your guardian's name as a thought or an audible sound during meditation. Or they may guide you to write it in your journal.

5. If you don't get a message from your guardian angel in your first meditation, don't worry. You may not be ready to receive it yet, but it is coming. It will probably come through unexpectedly, like in a song or on a license plate.

There are other ways to interact, work with angels, and use their protective powers. Below are a few.

Get to Know the Angel

The first step toward harnessing an angel's energy is by getting to know them. Here is how to learn more about the angel you're working with:

1. Find a quiet space (preferably with a door you can close to shut out other people's energetic influences).

2. Sit comfortably, close your eyes, relax your mind, and get in touch with your intuition. Ask your intuition for the name of angels to help you with your current endeavors.

3. The angel's name will appear in your mind. If it doesn't, the angels are letting you choose who you want to work with. You may even name the angel yourself.

4. If you're invited to name an angel, choose a name that makes you feel protected and loved when you think of them. Their name should make you feel warm and peaceful and smile.

5. Write down the name of the angel you've summoned, so you can call them when needed.

6. Once you have their name, address the angel, ask how they can help you, how they will send you signals, and how you will know they'll protect you. Offer clues on how you want to be protected and contacted, too.

7. Using the angels' names will help you stay more connected to them and make them seem more real and available when you need protection.

Ask Them to Send You a Sign

Angels love sending messages to improve your life or remind you of their loving presence and protection. You can ask them to send you a sign of their protective energies by penning down this request in your journal, expressing it through prayer, asking for it in a spell or ritual, or meditating on your request. After asking for a sign of their protection, you must pay attention to your environment. Look for signs from the angels that you're no longer at risk of physical attacks. They could come in a prophetic dream, a fresh perspective on a problematic situation, or an unexpected opportunity or relationship.

Dedicating Something to Them

Feel free to dedicate songs, poems, or letters to angels. It doesn't matter who the author is. It could be the song you've heard on the radio or a poem you've recently read. All that matters is that the angel understands how you wish to communicate. Once they learn this, they will reassure you of their protection through these means. You could write them a letter or poem. This could be about wanting protection or healing, or expressing gratitude for angelic protection.

Prayer for Angelic Protection

The following prayer is a great tool to evoke your guardian angels. It's an excellent way to honor them and shows you're aware of their presence and will summon them if needed. Your guardian angel will help you ward off malicious affiliations threatening your spiritual well-being.

Instructions:

1. Go to your sacred space and light a candle for the guardian angel.
2. Take a deep breath to center yourself and eliminate distracting thoughts from your mind.
3. Focus on your intention of bringing angelic protection into your life, space, or that of your loved ones.
4. When you're ready, recite the following prayer:

   "My angel, my loving guardian,

   Defend (insert the name) in upcoming challenges,

   So, the good vibes won't be lost when facing negative influences.

   My guardian, you've been by my side throughout my life.

   May you guard me on all my journeys."

Psychic Protection with Archangels

This meditation opens the gate for effective energy cleansing to counteract psychic attacks and remove the remnants of toxic energies from your life. Through it, you can experience the shielding energy of Archangels, the most powerful spiritual protectors in the universe. For example, you can use it to summon Archangel Michael to eradicate all forms of fear and negativity from your life. Whichever archangel you choose to call on, this meditation will help you experience their empowering, guiding presence as they uplift your energies, enabling you to obtain spiritual health and well-being.

Instructions:

1. Find a comfortable place where you won't be disturbed for at least 30 minutes.

2. Close your eyes and deepen your breath to center your mind and ground yourself.

3. When relaxed, visualize your core desires (intent) like a bright sphere glowing with white light.

4. Focus on the sphere and enjoy the silence and peace it brings to your mind. Breathe in - as if trying to pull the calm deep into your body.

5. As you exhale deeply, let go of all other thoughts from your consciousness. Will the calming energy to flow inward, and don't let new thoughts intrude on your consciousness.

6. Allow your intent to transcend the space and imagine it has taken the form of a spacious temple. Visualize yourself stepping into the temple and observing how it looks, feels, and sounds.

7. The temple is your sacred space, where divine energies protect you. No other energy can enter without permission or draw yours out against your will. Here, you have all the power to protect yourself.

8. As you're exploring the temple, feel how the power from the temple radiates throughout your body. You feel security, calmness, love, and well-being.

9. Now, imagine your divine space transforming into an orb of spinning white light. Feel the orb vibrating and floating upward, taking you through space to the luminous horizon above you.

10. As you pass a luminous golden mass traveling toward a source of bright light, you feel enveloped with more love, protection, peace, and joy as energy particles uplift your energies.

11. Feel how the protective energies enter your body, humming like your heartbeat. If you feel guided toward certain thoughts and emotions, feel free to join and follow them.

12. For a moment, return to yourself, and let the newfound emotions wash over you. Return to your previous vision on your next inhale. See the archangel in front of you with his sacred sword by his side.

13. Imagine embracing the angel. They may ask you permission to empower you with protective energy. After granting permission, invite the archangel in, and let them scan your mind, body, and soul to see where you need the most protection.

14. They will identify and source negative energies; with their sword, they will cut through them, detaching them from your body and freeing you from their bonds. They will help you to eliminate the psychic attack remains and reassure you that from now on, one can manipulate your energy without your permission.

15. Breathe deeply and let the negative energies go, assimilating the changes as your energy is cleansed. Notice thoughts and feelings passing through you as the negative influences make their way out of your life.

16. Ask yourself questions related to these emotions. For example, ask yourself who you need to forgive if you feel resentment. To whoever comes to mind, grant forgiveness and replace it with love. If you fear someone negatively impacts your vibes, tell them they no longer have permission to access your energy. Release negative interaction you've engaged in with this person.

17. Slowly let the images go and feel the relief washing over you, intertwined in the waves of forgiveness. The archangel is empowering you with their protective energy. If you need additional help with spiritual healing, ask the archangel to bless you with healing energy.

18. Visualize yourself being enveloped with a white robe, held together with a purple chain - the symbol of the angel's protective powers.

19. The angel creates three glowing orbs of energy around you, each spinning in a different direction. They're connected to your energy; between them is a powerful energy field. Their directions can never be aligned, so no outside force can breach the field.

20. The orbs will watch over you and stand guard to ward off future attacks. They represent a connection to the archangel, who you can now call on more easily.

21. Return to your body and feel re-empowered by your reinforced psychic protection. With a centering breath, open your eyes and return to your life.

Angelic Sigil Magic

Sigils are images of symbols incorporated into different magical acts. They represent the goal or intention you want to manifest - angelic protection. As they are magical tools, sigils must be activated with a ritual. You can use premade angelic sigils or create your own by focusing on what you want to achieve with them and channeling your spiritual energy into that purpose. The energy of the angel to whom the symbol belongs maintains this energy.

Using Angelic Sigils

You must use the correct ritual to establish the line of communication when using angel-summoning sigils. You must choose the right angel for your intention, their association (days, candles, prayers), and the appropriate intention.

Here is a simple summoning spell for angelic protection:

1. On your sacred place, arrange your tools - an angelic sigil, a candle associated with the angel, and another candle to represent your intention (use one candle if your intent matches the angel's powers).

2. Light the candles(s) and take the paper with the charged sigil in your hands.

3. Holding the sigil close to your body, get into a comfortable position and relax, taking a few deep breaths.

4. Close your eyes and visualize the sigil in front of you. If you struggle with this step, you can keep your eyes open and deeply gaze at the sigil.

5. Once your focus is fully on the sigil and other thoughts are eliminated from your mind, state your intention out loud:

   "By the power of the angel whose energy is in this sigil,

   I ask for my wishes to be granted.

   May I and those around me be protected,

   And guide on the sacred path of angels."

6. After another deep breath, release the sigil's image and open your eyes (or put the paper with the sigil down) and return to your day-to-day activities.

If the angel you've called on through the sigil wants to send a message, they will do so soon. You may receive this message in your dreams by tapping into your intuition, realizing your intention, reading a book, or in situations or visions related to your angelic sigil spell.

You can summon the power of an angel through sigil magic. However, working with archangels is recommended if you need reinforcement in a specific field (like psychic protection from powerful negative energies). You can invoke them on the days associated with their favorite colors. For example, the Archangel Samuel is best summoned with a rose-colored candle on a Tuesday.

To summon your guardian angel, you'll need the day of the week they've been assigned to you - the day you were born. It is the best way to form a connection to your spiritual guide and use them to make things work in your favor.

Depending on the issue you're dealing with, you can summon the angel best representing your problem (and its solutions) according to their qualities and powers. For example, the Archangel Samuel governs spiritual elevation, protection, and peace, whereas if you need empowerment, faith, and courage to fend off negative energies, you'll need the powers of Archangel Michael.

Chapter 7: Stones, Plants, and Symbols of Protection

As the title implies, this chapter is dedicated to protective crystals, protective plants, and symbols of protection. It lists the most common and potent crystals, plants, and protection symbols, with their spiritual purpose and suggestions for using them for protection purposes. You'll learn to create and charge your sigils of protection.

Protective Crystals

Crystals can help keep you connected to your mind, body, and soul.

Using crystals is a wonderful way of keeping connected to your mind, body, soul, and psychic energies. Using true crystals is recommended, as these were formed from natural ingredients and are a great way to incorporate nature into your daily life. Crystals vibrate at different frequencies. For example, the vibes of some stones can help you fend off psychic attacks. Others will help you flush out energy that is not serving you.

While certain crystals are better for psychic protection than others, the best stones are those you're drawn to. The crystal's energy will feel inviting to you, connecting with your energy. It can make you pause, learn to raise your vibrations, and protect yourself. Below are a few crystals with pronounced protective energies.

Black Tourmaline

Black tourmaline can be an incredibly potent protector for your aura. Its energy has grounding and soothing effects. Its energy provides calming and anchoring qualities. It can stop harmful energy that someone else is sending your way. Negative thinking patterns, often associated with psychic attacks, can be banished by the healing energies of this black stone. For instance, unfavorable influences can make you experience severe anxiety. Black tourmaline has the power to calm your mind, push away worry-filled thoughts, and give you the confidence you once had. Black tourmaline is one of the best crystals to add to your collection if you want to block out all the negative energy from your life, your environment, and the lives of others around you.

The best way to use black tourmaline for protection is during meditation. While holding the stone, you only need to consider what you wish to be protected from. Alternatively, you can wear black tourmaline if you struggle with persistently pessimistic thoughts, anxiety, or dread of harmful energy or keep it in your pocket. It creates a protective energy bubble around you.

Obsidian

The second black gemstone on this list, obsidian, absorbs negative energy like the color black incorporates all other colors. When you are afflicted by negative energy, this crystal can help you to overcome those moments. When you are experiencing negative vibrations that are weighing you down with heavy thoughts, it can help you to find clarity. Uncomfortable truths about your emotions and interpersonal connections may come to light. It can help you identify anything another person is trying to conceal from you.

Since it absorbs all negative energy around you, obsidian is not a stone you can always wear, and it must be cleansed often. However, you can place it around your home. Setting this stone by entryways blocks negative energy threatening to enter your space, halting it in its tracks. By absorbing these negative energy vibrations and returning them as positive ones, obsidian will shield your home and everyone inside from that negative energy.

Amethyst

Amethyst can help with psychic shielding while being mostly recognized for relieving stomach aches and other stress-related ailments. This purple stone promotes tranquil, calming energy and protects against overpowering feelings that cause anxiety and despair. Amethyst provides emotional and spiritual protection by stabilizing mental health. It helps you become more conscious of bad energy and the necessity to eliminate it from your life.

Amethyst can be put to many different uses. You can keep it near where you frequently are, wear it as a charm on a bracelet or necklace, or keep it in your pocket. Placing the stone under your pillow as you sleep will provide additional protection for dream work and spiritual contact, even when your conscious mind is asleep.

Clear Quartz

Due to its innate ability to connect with other natural energies, clear quartz can take on the energy of other crystals near it. You can use clear quartz to amplify the energy of a protective crystal you're using. Besides manifesting more protection in your life, this stone can be used for purification. Clear quartz cleanses energy and empowers your natural protective abilities by flushing out negative vibes from your mind, body, and soul.

If you want to use it as a cleansing stone, wear clear quartz as a charm or put it in your pocket. If you want to amplify the potency of other crystals, use them alongside in rituals and spells. For example, you can move it up and down in front of your body or hold it close to your heart and over another crystal while casting a protection spell. It will shield your energy and release negative vibes from the body.

Pyrite

Pyrite is a golden crystal guarding your energy against negative vibes. If you have been to a crystal shop, you have probably seen this beauty. Its golden color manifests abundance and boosts confidence, which is handy when increasing your psychic protection. This stone helps you release negativity and manifest positive changes in your life by making you more confident about protecting yourself from outside influences.

Pyrite is incredibly powerful and can be effective regardless of how you use it. Whether you want to keep it in your bag or pocket or put it in the entryways of your home or office - it will protect you. If you want to wear it or keep it close to your body, you must cleanse it often with clear quartz so it can shield you wherever you go.

Smithsonite

Smithsonite is not only beautiful, but it's also the stone with the most serene energy. Its vibrations can help calm the emotions caused by negative vibes emanating from other people. It can center you, helping you relax and focus on erecting the necessary protection against harmful influences.

Smithsonite is best used for protecting your home or office space. Place it in a special place (like an altar or other sacred area) to help you ward off unhealthy energies from your home. Or keep it in your drawer at the office, reminding you of its protective powers on a stressful day with toxic coworkers.

Black Jade

Another black stone on the list is black jade. It can help you connect with your intuition and learn which people to avoid. Your intuition knows who emanates negative vibes or in which situations you are most likely to be affected. Black jade will help you identify where negativity enters your life and eliminate the root of your energy issues.

You can use black jade as a personal (energy) guardian and take it with you wherever you go, wearing it as a charm or keeping it in your pocket. It will be particularly effective when you meet new people, travel to new places, or venture into new experiences.

Protective Plants

Like natural stones, plants are connected to nature and its universal power that provides healing and connects all living beings. You use natural energy to protect yourself from physical attacks and cleanse your energy. Due to this, placing plants in certain areas of your home or workspace has plenty of benefits on your vibrations. Looking at greenery reduces stress, improves mood, and eliminates other symptoms of toxic energetic influences. Plants enable you to defend yourself against bad energies by improving your physical and mental health. Plants give out positive energy and eliminate toxic energies from their surroundings.

Moreover, plants produce immense amounts of oxygen, which is good for the environment. All living beings that thrive on oxygen will be filled with more positive energy, including people. The more positive vibes in the environment, the more sources you'll have to tap into when you need an added boost of good vibes to fend off toxic influences. Here are plants for spiritual protection:

Basil

The deep green leaves of basil emanate plenty of positive energy. They have antioxidant properties, which improve the metabolism of all beings laced with positive energy. It increases the positive energy in your environment and is a powerful aid in spiritual protection.

You can use basil in many ways for psychic protection. For example, you can use them to anoint candles for protective spells and rituals. Put dried basil in a satchel (with other protective herbs) and place it under your pillow. Or, you can keep a pot of basil plant on a windowsill to block out negative energies from your home.

Aloe Vera

The aloe vera plant is of the most common houseplants for psychic protection, albeit its use is often unintentional. Many people know of this plant's healing, soothing, and stress-relieving properties. However, these can also protect your aura.

Since aloe vera can survive any weather, you can keep it anywhere in your home or workplace. Placing the plant near where you spend most time will fill you with plenty of positive vibes and flush out negative energy. Take advantage of its healing and cleansing properties by creating homemade lotions for added protection.

Sage

The sage plant is another herb to help you eliminate toxic energy from your surroundings. It enables you to flush out negative emotions (including anger and fear) caused by bad vibes.

Plant sage in small pots, and place them in your home where you need the most protection. You can use dried sage for cleansing rituals like ritual baths or smudging. The former is great for flushing out negative influences from your body, while the latter eliminates them from your surroundings. Or, you can use the dried herb as anointment in protective rituals and ceremonies, place it under your pillow in a satchel, or keep it with you as a talisman.

Vetiver

Vetiver is another houseplant linked to improving mental health; it elevates spiritual protection. Vetiver encourages positive energy flow and helps reduce toxic energy flow. Its calming aurora helps relax your mind and improves sleep, enhancing your ability to ward off negative influences. You can place vetiver anywhere you need the most protection.

Lavender

Lavender's soothing aroma helps reduce stress, boosts relaxation, and flushes out toxic energies from your body. Besides relieving symptoms of stress and depression, lavender is also great for spiritual protection. Its oils eliminate negative vibes from the environment and encourage the flow of positive energies.

Lavender can be used in oil, fresh, or dried. For example, use dried lavender in a spiritual cleansing bath or smudging. Lavender oil and fresh flowers can be used in purification rituals, contributing to the accumulation of positive energy to protect you from toxic vibes.

Jasmine

Jasmine can bring positive energy into romantic or close familial relationships. Place this plant anywhere around your house to surround everyone with good vibes. It is particularly effective if you believe someone is trying to cause a rift in your relationship with their negative vibes.

Thyme

Thyme is another aromatic herb known to boost vibes. It can bring you good luck and confidence in your abilities. Like sage, you can use dry thyme in rites and spells to fight off negative energy. Or, incorporate it into cleansing rituals, like baths and smudging. Dried or fresh thyme near your bed (including under your pillow) helps improve sleep and spiritual communication through sleep and wards off nightmares.

Peace Lily

The peace lily boosts positive energy flow around your home or office space, helping protect yourself from negative influences in your private and professional life. The plant purifies the air, effectively reducing headaches and other symptoms of stress caused by toxic energies. Place it anywhere with little sunlight. It will charge itself and your surroundings with even more protective energy.

Jade Plant

Like the peace lily, the jade plant helps improve your mood by eliminating negative energies from your environment. It gives you more confidence to defend yourself and your loved ones from psychic attacks. Keep the jade plant at the home's entrance, and all those inside it will be protected.

Symbols of Protection

Symbols have been used for spiritual protection since ancient times. All cultures employ some symbolism during protective spells and rituals. Below are a few of the most powerful symbols of psychic protection.

Triquetra

The triquetra, known as the trinity knot, is one of the oldest protective symbols. It consists of three interlaced arcs, with loops knotted together, forming a triangle. The triquetra has been used in pagan cultures and Celtic fold magic, but its uses have been traced to Asian regions. In Celtic mythology, the triquetra denotes the three natural realms - the sky, the sea, and the earth.

The symbol can represent your body's physical, mental, and spiritual states. Hence, it's great for overall spiritual protection. You can wear the triquetra as a charm or keep it close to your body to protect you on the go. Or, incorporate it into rituals and spells when you need added reinforcement to ward off toxic influences.

Turtle

Due to their long lifespan, turtles are lucky charms in many cultures. The animal has hard body armor, which symbolizes spiritual strength and resilience. The turtle signifies a power for protection against harmful energies. It reminds you that you can overcome any obstacle as long as you can ward off toxic vibes. Even if your goal might seem far away, by slowly building your spiritual energies, you'll reach it. No matter how many hurdles you face, a turtle symbol will help you stay motivated and determined to reach your goals. The best way to use this symbol for psychic protection is to wear it as an amulet.

Helm of Awe

This protection symbol comes from Norse mythology, associated with protection against enemies. Viking tribes painted this symbol on their bodies before battle to invite good luck and protection. Besides offering protection against toxic energies, the helm of awe is used to dissipate fears. It's depicted as eight tridents centered on a core area, shielding it from evil. It's a reminder that no matter how potent the negative energy is, you will always be protected by it. This symbol helps suppress your fears, giving you confidence in your choices and abilities to defend your aura from negative influences. You can incorporate it into protective rituals and spells, or wear it as a charm or talisman for an added protection layer when heading onto uncharted territories, like meeting new people and situations.

The Evil Eye

The evil eye is another commonly used and revered protection symbol used globally. Known as *nazar*, the evil eye symbol is associated with inner sight. It improves self-awareness and draws attention to areas that need protection. The symbol is depicted as a blue-and-white picture of an eye.

The symbol can repel negative energies, especially if worn as jewelry, charm, or talisman. It protects you from harmful influences, including those emanating from people wishing you bad luck and misfortune. It replies to jealous thoughts and any associated bad vibes. Incorporate it into your decor and furniture to protect your home.

Dragonfly

The dragonfly is known for its transformative abilities. It's a powerful symbol of self-actualization and spiritual elevation. With spiritual advancement comes a higher ability to ward off negative vibes.

Dragonflies are connected to fire and water energy, the duality reminding you of the balance of the opposing aspects in your life. They are associated with new beginnings and goals in your personal and professional life.

Using a dragonfly symbol for spiritual protection can help you invite more positive energy into your life, replacing negativity. It can inspire you to look at the bright side of every situation (no matter how challenging) rather than being consumed by negative influences.

Wear the symbol as a charm or talisman daily to brighten up your life and become more confident in protecting your spiritual energies. It will help you prosper in your spiritual journey, adding light and happiness to your life.

How to Create and Charge Symbols

You can create your own signs (sigils) for protection. All you need is a sheet of paper, a pencil, and a candle (in color representing your intention) to make your sigils.

Instructions:

1. Write the reason for your sigil on the paper. For example, you can pen down your need for protection from a spiritual guide. Write it as something you've already achieved rather than something you wish to achieve.

2. Cross out all the vowels and consonants appearing more than once in your writing. Create a sentence with the remaining letters. Then, create a symbol incorporating each word's first letter.

3. Activate the sigil by writing it on another piece of paper while focusing on your intention. Put the sigil aside; don't think about it until you need it. Alternatively, you can burn the paper with the sigil on it.

4. You can use the sigil to summon protective energy. For example, if you're calling on a protective power of an angel, the sigil will help get in touch with the angel to whom the symbol belongs and maintain this energy.

After activating the sigil, you must charge your symbol to empower it with protective energy. You can do this by:

- Storing it somewhere meaningful
- Carving it into a candle and lighting it
- Drawing a protective sigil on your body
- Tracing a sigil in the air and visualizing its dissipation
- Drawing a sigil into your food and eating it

Chapter 8: Breaking Curses, Hexes, and Attachments

This chapter enlists several spells and rituals to defend against curses, hexes, and unwanted attachments and relationships. It explains curses and hexes, their differences, why they happen, and how to identify if you are a victim of one.

Curses and Hexes

Curses and hexes are spells that can bring harm to a target.
https://unsplash.com/photos/x69K221AGHw?utm_source=unsplash&utm_medium=referral&utm_content=creditShareLink

Hexes are simple negativity-inducing spells cast by a person with evil intent. Depending on how they are cast, hex spells can be more formal than curses. Sometimes they require a handy spell, while at other times, they need a complicated ritual. It depends on how much the person wishes to harm their target. However, even the most evil-intentioned and potent hexes can be broken.

A curse is also a spell that hurts its target by bringing bad luck, misfortune, illness, financial hardship, and other hurdles into their life. There are two primary curses: The chaos curse, which leads to random negative events, and the entropy curse, which targets a person or several people and increases the likelihood of being afflicted by negative vibes. Curses can be personal or generational.

The number of different curses and hexes used by witches is vast, but a few common ones are used to impart the same sentiments. For example, the evil eye is caused by envy, hatred, jealousy, malice, anger, and resentment. Although there are several evil eyes, they all have one thing in common - they are born from a magic spell cast by someone who wants to harm you.

How to Identify if You're a Victim of a Curse or Hex

Curses and hexes are more common than you may realize. Here are tips on how to recognize if you're a victim of a curse or hex:

1. The feeling of defeat, discouragement, and depression: You feel completing even the simplest task seems hopeless and overwhelming, and you're constantly disappointed in yourself or feel like giving up on everything.

2. You're plagued by physical fatigue, constantly get sick, or generally feel a lack of energy or motivation.

3. You lack a desire for spiritual development: You may have difficulty praying, connecting to spiritual guides, or performing practices for spiritual enlightenment.

4. Loss of faith: You may feel let down by your spirit guides – and they're now punishing you.

5. A negative view on life: You could be wrestling with anxious thoughts, worries, or fears or feel nobody cares for you.

6. Consider returning to old practices regardless of how harmful they were to your spiritual health. Curses can cause you to consider moving backward instead of forward with your life.

7. Reopening old emotional wounds: Even if you believe you've closed a painful chapter of your life, a curse or hex can reopen them, making you deal with the hurt all over again.

8. Feeling guilt, shame, and condemnation constantly: You may feel your thoughts, emotions, and actions are not good enough for you to be accepted.

9. Feeling rejected, lonely, and thinking you don't belong: You feel no one understands your feelings, so you cannot belong anywhere.

10. Confusion over belief and ideas: Psychic attacks can cause you to doubt your beliefs and question your reality.

Curse or Hex Removal with Lemon and Sea Salt

This simple curse or hex removal ritual uses salt's spiritual cleansing properties and lemon's revitalizing energy. It banishes negativity from inside and around your body. Don't use it if you have open wounds or cuts.

Ingredients:
- A lemon
- Sea salt

Instructions:

1. Cut your lemon in half, and cover each half with sea salt.

2. Wipe the lemons over your body, one half at a time. Cleanse your aura and channel the toxic energy brought on by a curse or hex into the lemon.

3. Throw away the lemon when you have finished. Otherwise, the bad energy continues lingering around you.

4. You should feel better a few hours after the ritual. However, it's best to repeat it for at least a week. You can do it as long as you feel the toxic energies and other effects of curses around you.

Salt Water Bath to Break a Hex

Magical baths are spells for breaking curses and hexes. It's an excellent spiritual cleansing. It helps break off the negative energy flow directed toward you and replenishes its void with plenty of positive vibes. For the best effects, perform this ritual at night, during the waning moon phase. The latter is associated with banishing, withdrawing, and eliminating negative things from a person's life or space. The sea (and, by extension, sea salt) is associated with the moon, so this ritual creates a powerful link between a banishing bath and lunar magick.

Ingredients:

- 1 cup of sea salt
- 1 cup of Epsom salts
- A glass of water
- 1/4 cup of baking soda

Instructions:

1. Draw water into your bathtub and add the baking soda and salts to the bathwater. Place the glass of water on the tub's rim.

2. Stir the water counterclockwise to combine the ingredients.

3. Before getting into the bath, hold your hands in a prayer position and close your eyes.

4. Visualize the water being filled and surrounded with an orb of bright, white light.

5. Get in the tub and soak for at least 30 minutes.

6. While it helps remove negative energy deep within you, soaking in salty water can be very dehydrating. Feel free to sip from the glass of water to stay hydrated.

7. Once you have finished soaking, exit the tub and dry off.

8. Open your window, and ask the waning moon to finish cleansing you of curses and hexes during the night.

Calling On Spiritual Guides to Banish Negative Energy

Banishing curses can be as simple as asking your spiritual guides to boost your psychic protection. Whether you prefer to work with deities, angels, ancestral spirituals, or other guides, praying to them can help you explore negativity in your life. Whether you were cursed or hexed by a person's malicious intent or an evil spirit, your spirit guides, guardian angels, deities, and ancestral spirits won't hesitate to help you. They can help you identify the source of the bad magic, remove it, direct it back to the spell-caster, and bless you with positivity. If the entity can't help you, it will direct your message to a more powerful one. For example, if your guardian angel can't help by removing your curse or protecting you against it, they will advise you to call on an archangel to help you.

Ingredients:

- A candle associated with the deity, angel, or spirit you're summoning
- A representation of the deity, angel, or spirit you're summoning
- A prayer addressed to the deity, angel, or spirit you're summoning

Instructions:

1. Light the candle and assume a relaxed position in front of your altar, shrine, or other sacred space. It helps if this space is dedicated to the being you're summoning.

2. Focusing on your intent, recite the prayer. You can repeat it several times if you wish. Meditate on your intent after you've finished praying.

3. Thank the entity you summoned for their attention and the blessing they'll provide you with in the future.

4. Repeat your prayer the next day. Working the prayer into your everyday life enables you to build a strong bond with the entities you're addressing. The stronger the relationship, and the more dedicated you are to it, the more this entity will help you repeal or break curses and hexes.

A Crystal Wand Ritual for Spiritual Cleansing

Crystal wands are excellent tools for cleansing your body, home, or another space of negative energy curses and hexes. Alternatively, use crystals instead of crystals wands. The rituals also use other crystals to replenish positive energy. Choose the stone that suits your needs best and replaces negativity with positivity in all the right places. For example, after eliminating the curse or hex's energy from your professional space, use stones that bring good luck and fortune. If you've eliminated the person who affected your self-esteem's energy, you'll need crystals that help you nurture self-love.

Ingredients:

- A crystal that absorbs or counteracts negative energy
- A crystal to fill in the space or yourself with positivity

Instructions:

1. Stand by an open window so the negative energy can leave you and your space as soon as possible. Even if you're only cleansing your space, don't forget to open the windows so the bad vibes have somewhere to go. Otherwise, they will just infect your space and you instead of leaving.

2. In one motion, sweep the crystal (or crystal wand) over your body. Then, move the crystal toward the window, directing the toxic energy away from you and out the window. Do this if you want to eliminate negative influences from your person.

3. Start further from the window to remove curses, hexes, or other malicious vibes from a space. Slowly advancing, move your crystal toward the window several times. When you reach the window, move the crystal as if directing the energy outside.

4. Once you've dispelled the negative energies from your person or space, close your window and take a positivity-bringing crystal. If you've cleansed yourself, sweep the crystal over your body, focusing on filling yourself with positivity.

5. If you've cleansed your space, walk around with the second crystal, focusing on the same intention.

Cleansing Ritual to Remove Curses

This cleansing ritual with eggs will help you remove the evil eye and other common curses from your person. It uses the egg as a vessel for the toxic energy caused by the curse. The curse is drawn away from the person and channeled into the egg.

Ingredients:

- An egg
- A candle (optional)
- A jar

• Water

Instructions:

1.Stand in front of your altar or sacred space with the egg in your hands.

2.Calm your mind and focus on your intention. If you work with deities or spiritual guides, call on them to empower and help you put the curse into the egg.

3.Rub the egg over your body, focusing on areas where you feel discomfort or pain, which could indicate the accumulation of negative energies.

4.You may feel chills around parts of your body, and this is a good sign. It means the egg is drawing negativity from you.

5.Then say the following three times:

6."May all the curses leave my body, mind, and soul, now."

7.Once you feel the egg has absorbed all the negative energies, fill the jar with water and crack the egg into it.

8.Try to read the egg to see the source of the curse. Pay attention to the different shapes, like flowers, people, and other characteristics you can discern as the egg mixes with the water.

9.Once you've finished observing the egg-water mixture, flush it down the toilet.

A Magical Poppet to Banish Bad Magic

Using a poppet (a small doll made from cloth, clay, wood, wax, paper, or other material), you can redirect energy from a person or draw it toward them. Besides people, poppets can represent animals and inanimate objects. Sometimes, poets can embody the soul of a person who died and left a curse or hex behind or was cursed or hexed themselves before death. The spell uses the poppet to represent you or your loved ones and redirect toxic energies directed at you or another person.

Ingredients:

• A poppet - you can buy or make one. For example, you can sew a cotton doll and stuff it with items representing the person you want to protect.

• More items representing you or another person you want to protect (pictures, trinkets, or anything else tied to the person's energy)

• A mirror

Instructions:

1. Take the poppet and the other items to the mirror and hold the doll facing the mirror. If the spell is for you, look into the poppets eyes, and say:

   "As I look into this doll's eye, I become at one with it.

   All evil I may receive will go into this doll,

   And I will be spared from toxic energies."

2. If the spell is for someone else, you can have the person with you and have them repeat the above chant. Or, if you're working remotely, say:

   "This doll is now (the person's name).

   May they be protected from evil,

   As their doppelganger absorbs any toxic energies."

3. Leave the doll in a safe place and let it soak up the negative energies (hexes and ill intent) sent your way or the way of the person you want to protect.

4. If you or the other person have experienced signs of being cursed or hexed, these signs will soon go away.

A Candle Ritual to Remove Evil Forces from Your Environment

This candle magic ritual mixes the power of a black and a white candle. The first is associated with evil, death, and darkness. It denotes the absence of light and is often used to represent night, mourning, and grief. The white candle embodies purity, spirituality, innocence, light, goodness, truth, harmony, peace, love, unity, and balance. White is linked to the stars, moon, angels, and soul. Combining these colors, you can absorb negative forces from your space and replace them with positive vibes.

Ingredients:

• A small white candle
• A small black candle

Instructions:

1. Place the white and a black candle in front of you on your altar or other sacred space. Light them.

2. Calm your mind and say a prayer of gratitude for the positivity in your life to reinforce your intent to chase away negativity.

3. Focus on what your wish to eliminate from your space (your home or workplace) and what you want this space to be filled with.

4. Leave the candles to burn down completely. Avoid blowing them out because it could cause your spell to be disrupted. It's best to perform this spell late in the afternoon when you have plenty of time to supervise the candles before going to bed.

Freezing Spell for Unwanted Attachments

Freezing or souring is used to freeze someone out of your life. You can use them on people who cause you energetic blockages or taint your energy with their toxic vibes. These could be your enemies, people who spread gossip about you while pretending to care about you, or anyone envious of your successes. Don't use it on people you wish to reconcile with later and don't cast the spell in anger. Traditionally you would use salt or vinegar for the spell. Salt can help you make a person's hurtful words bitter in their mouth, severing your connection to them. Vinegar will sour the person, so they'll stop attaching their negative vibes to yours.

Ingredients:

- Sealable container (freezer bag, jar, etc.).
- Charged water (salt or vinegar water) – alternatively, use tap water. However, it will make the spell less effective.
- Totem - to represent the person (or situation you encounter this person) to freeze. It could be a photograph of them, their belongings, or their name on a piece of paper.
- Fruit and vegetables.
- Details of the situations written on paper (in case you are detaching yourself from unhealthy situations).
- Black candle wax - for sealing (optional).
- Black pepper or chili flakes (optional, for making the person's lies or gossip burn in their mouth).

Instructions:

1. Prepare the totem and the written details of the situation (if using any) on your altar, shrine, or other sacred space.

2. Light the black candle. Place the totem (and the paper with the details) in the empty container.

3. Put the fruit and vegetables into the container. If you're using chili or pepper flakes, add them.

4. Fill the container with salt or vinegar water. Close the container.

5. Seal the container by dripping black candle wax on the opening or lid. As you do this, meditate on your intention. Imagine your connection to this person being severed and them disappearing from your life. Revere on the feeling of satisfaction this image brings you.

6. Alternatively, wrap the container in aluminum foil. Ensure the foil's shiny side faces inward so the person's negative energy bounces back to them. You could combine both techniques by sealing the container with wax, then wrapping it in foil for added spell potency.

7. Put the container in the freezer. Leave it there for as long as required for the spell to take effect.

8. Once the spell is complete, remove the container from the freezer, toss its contents into the trash, or leave them in a bin near a crossroads. These options are the safest when the person has been successfully frozen out of your life.

9. Alternatively, leave the container in the freezer and forget about it. It signals that you cannot be bothered to toss it out because the person doesn't deserve your energy thinking of them.

10. If the spell hasn't worked or the person has reappeared in your life, don't toss out the spell. You must recharge it instead. Remove the container from the freezer, thaw it for a few days, and return it to the freezer after meditating on your intention.

11. If you're dealing with a particularly strong attachment, repeat the above process every few days to intensify the spell's power. Continue until the person stops contacting you, gossiping about you, or doing anything against you for good.

Hexes and curses can be broken, regardless of the intent's strength. Use your entities' power to help you break free from a spell.

Chapter 9: Shielding Yourself and Your Loved Ones

If only you could always be surrounded by positivity without harmful influences or energies seeping into your life. However, this isn't realistic. There is no escape from the negativity. Psychic attacks can occur anytime and anywhere, either by accident or on purpose. In other words, you can't control where or how you get these attacks, but you can shield yourself and your family from them.

This chapter provides multiple protection rituals, tips, and techniques to keep yourself and your loved ones safe.

Remember, perform preparation and cleansing rituals before you practice any technique.

Rituals can be used to protect yourself and your loved ones from harm.

Clearing Ceremony

A clearing ceremony is an effective technique against psychic attacks. It involves burning sage, where the smoke releases dark energy from your body and shields you from future negative influences.

Ingredients:
- Sage smudge stick
- Lavender or sandalwood

Instructions:
1. Put the sage and lavender in the same bundle.
2. Light the herbs with a match, blow out the fire, and place them in a large bowl.
3. Set the intention to shield yourself from dark influences and psychic attacks. You can say a prayer, *"I am protecting myself from the dark forces holding power over me."*
4. Sit on the floor and look up to ask the universe to give you strength and wisdom against these dark forces.
5. Look down at the ground beneath you and feel your connection with Mother Earth. Thank her for the blessings she bestows on you and for allowing you to eliminate these attacks.
6. Cleanse yourself with the sage and let the smoke wash away the negativity.
7. Close your eyes and visualize a protective circle surrounding you, keeping you safe.

You can perform this ritual at your office to protect yourself against psychic attacks in the workplace.

Journaling

Not all dreams are messages from your subconscious. You can experience psychic attacks in your sleep as nightmares or night terrors. People are always vulnerable in the dream world since they have no control over their actions or environment.

Many people don't pay attention to their dreams, while others don't remember them, so you may not be aware that you are experiencing these attacks in your sleep. You may wake up feeling exhausted or stressed, but you don't know why, or you remember your nightmare but don't think much about it.

Tracking your dreams can protect you from psychic attacks while you sleep. Keep a journal by your bedside and write down all your dreams and nightmares when you first wake up before you forget them. Write how you felt in these dreams, like fear, sadness, or anger, and if these emotions stay with you after you wake up.

If you struggle with recalling your dreams, every night before you go to sleep, pray to the universe to help you remember them. Seek the protection of your guardian angels or ancestors to keep you safe in the dream world when you are alone and helpless. Ask them to bless you with happy and light dreams, filling you with love and comfort. You could listen to binaural beats while falling asleep, listening to two tones with different frequencies in each ear. This method leads the brain to create the illusion of a third tone which improves your memory and attention and makes you relax.

Before sleeping, repeat this mantra;

"Dear spirit guides, please provide me with guidance
and protection in the dream world."

Cut the Cord and Earth Cording

You can regularly perform these effective and simple techniques. Practice Earth cording in the morning and cord cutting at night.

Ingredients: A bowl of salt water

Instructions:

1. Before you sleep, sit in your bed, close your eyes, and visualize a cord coming out of your belly connecting you to someone or thing (it can be the person attacking your energy or an object you believe is causing psychic attacks).

2. Pretend your fingers are scissors and cut the cord between you and the negative energy source impacting your life. If there is more than one person or object behind these attacks, imagine multiple cords coming out of each of your seven chakras connecting you to them, and cut each individually.

3. Repeat this affirmation while cutting the cords:

"I release energetic attachments to protect myself
from negativity and psychic attacks."

4. After cutting the cords, visualize placing them in the saltwater bowl.

Earth Cording Instructions:

1. In the morning, after you wake up, sit on the ground comfortably and close your eyes.

2. Visualize a cord or more coming out of your belly and connecting you to the Earth. The cords are nurturing, flexible, and strong. You are at one with the Earth, which sustains and protects you. Nothing and no one is strong enough to cut these cords or separate you from Mother Earth.

Strengthen Your Aura

Instructions:

1. Stand in a quiet place without distractions, close your eyes, and breathe in and out deeply.

2. Imagine the colors of each of your seven chakras surrounding you like wheels.

3. Imagine the wheels expanding with every breath until they merge, creating a large colorful circle around you and shielding you from external energies.

4. You are in control of your auric field, and nothing can get in or out without your permission.

5. Repeat this mantra during the visualization, *"I only allow positive vibes in and prevent negativity from coming near me."*

Let Light Surround You

Instructions:

1. Sit comfortably and visualize your heart and the space around it as a white flame.

2. Take deep breaths and imagine the flame growing with every breath until it becomes a big circle surrounding and shielding you.

3. The white light is coming out of you and is part of your being. You are protecting yourself, and this makes you powerful.

4. Repeat this mantra, *"I am guided and protected. I am the light, and nothing can touch me."*

Meditation Technique #1

Instructions:

1. Sit in a quiet room with no distractions.

2. Get comfortable and relax your body and mind.

3. Close your eyes and take a few deep breaths until your mind is clear.

4. Imagine a bubble of golden energy surrounding you.

5. The bubble is transparent and acts as a shield against negative energy.

6. Imagine dark, negative energy coming toward you, but the protective shield prevents it from getting in.

7. Now, visualize positive and loving energy approaching you and filling the golden bubble.

8. Repeat these steps until you feel comfortable and believe you are protected. The golden bubble is filled with positive energy nourishing you and is strong enough to defend against psychic attacks.

Meditation Technique #2

Instructions:

1. Find a quiet space with no distractions.

2. Lie down and close your eyes.

3. Breathe deeply and take a few minutes to enjoy the peace and quiet.

4. Let go of all your expectations, worries, anxieties, and fears.

5. Think positive thoughts, and let them fill you with joy, compassion, and gratitude.

6. Take a deep breath and let out a long sigh.

7. Scan your body to assess your energy.

8. Breathe in positivity and breathe out negativity for a couple of minutes.

9. Pause for a minute.

10. Focus on your crown chakra (the top of your head).

11. Visualize your energy as a bright light shining over the top of your head.

12. Now, the light is surrounding you, and you feel safe.

13. Spend time focusing on the light.

14. It isn't the light protecting you; it merely acts as your boundary, reminding you that you are in control. You will not allow negative entities into your personal space.

15. Imagine the light getting closer and closer to your body until it becomes an extra layer of skin.

16. Think of the energy you want to embrace, like empowerment or nourishment.

17. Pause for a minute.

18. Think of the energy you want to shield yourself from, like negative thoughts, guilt, or shame.

19. Allow yourself to control your energy, as now you know what you will let in and what you will prevent from coming near you.

20. You are now fully aware of your energy and will notice if it changes or is under attack.

21. Your shield is a part of you, so always keep it up. It prevents people from crossing a line and attacking your energy.

22. Practice this meditation every morning.

Visualization

Instructions:

1. Sit in a comfortable position or lie down in a quiet room.

2. Place pink rose quartz around you or hold one in your hand.

3. Take a few deep breaths and remain quiet for a while.

4. Let go of the tension and stress until you feel calm and relaxed.

5. Focus on creating a blue protective shield.

6. Set an intention. Say:

"I intend to create a protective shield
of divine love and light."

7. Imagine a wall of mirrors surrounding you facing outward. So, if you are under a psychic attack, the negative energy will be

reflected outward.

8. Your shield is sealed to prevent unwanted energy from getting to you.

9. Set an intention for only love and joy to get through, and you will only send positive vibes out to the universe.

10.   You are inside the shield. Imagine the pink rose quartz's energy surrounding and embracing you.

11.   Feel the shield around you as if it's giving you a big hug. Stay with it for a while and repeat your intention.

Steer Clear from Negative People

If you know the people who attack your energy, avoid them as much as possible. All these methods are powerful enough to protect you. However, like any shield, it can weaken with constant exposure to negativity. If you feel your aura or energy altering around certain people, limit your interactions with them. Cut them off if possible, or spend less time with them. However, if this is someone you have to interact with daily, like a family member or your boss, keep your shield up and wear a protective gemstone or symbol whenever you are around them. Place a protective crystal or plant on your desk if this is someone you work with.

Chanting

Chanting is another powerful defense against psychic attacks. Create a chant reflecting your desire for the universe to protect you, write it on your phone, and read it a few times during the day. If you can't think of a chant, use this one or something similar.

"Spirits of the ancestors, guardian angels, and divine universe,

I am grateful for the cleansing white light you have bestowed upon me, healing me from all the darkness and negativity. I ask for your help and guidance to release everything that is not serving me and bringing me harm. Please protect my aura and space and only allow loving light and energy to flow through me. I pray you will send me healing energy to shield me.

Thank you for all your blessings."

Affirmations

- I am protected by a white light.

- I only attract positive energy, and negativity has no power over me.
- Positive thoughts and energy constantly surround me.
- My protective shield prevents negative thoughts from coming my way.
- I am filled with light healing me from negativity.
- I am surrounded by happiness and won't allow negative vibes into my space.
- I am a force of light and love; nothing can touch me.
- I am connected to Mother Earth; she protects me from dark energies.
- I release negative energy to Mother Earth and only embrace positive vibes.
- I am strong. Psychic attacks don't bother me.
- I am a walking shield, and negative energy can't reach me.
- My body is filled with positivity; there is no space for dark energies.
- My shield is powerful. Nothing and no one can get through.
- I am in control of my auric field and will not allow anyone or anything to alter my aura.
- I am surrounded by a powerful protective field.
- I will not allow (name person) negative influences to get to me.
- (Name person) has no power over me.
- (Name person) isn't allowed in my space.
- (Name person) can't impact my energy.
- I will not allow anyone to influence me.
- I am protected against other people's bad intentions.
- I always find my power and will not let anyone take it from me.
- I release all the energies not belonging to me.
- My energy is mine; no one can alter it or take it from me.
- I send positive vibes to the universe and receive good vibes back.
- I am bringing back my strength.
- I call back the energy taken from me.
- I send back the foreign energies not serving me.

- Divine protection is blessing my psychic abilities.
- My mind is safe from psychic attacks.
- My psychic powers are growing, and I control them.
- My shield is strong, psychic attacks bounce off it, and nothing can penetrate it.
- My energy field is protected with divine light, preventing negative influences from reaching me.
- I am protected by a bubble of light; it doesn't allow negativity to touch me.
- I protect my mind from psychic attacks.
- The universe is powerful and protects me against psychic attacks.
- Divine protection protects my body, mind, and spirit from negative influences.
- My guardian angel protects my body and soul.
- My guardian angel is by my side, shielding me from psychic attacks.
- Darkness cannot penetrate my protective shield.
- My guardian angel is keeping me safe.
- I embrace the protection of my spirit guides.

Affirmations to Protect Your Children, Pets, and Loved Ones

- My children are my only priority, and I will keep them safe.
- I place a force field around my family; nothing can penetrate it.
- My pets are surrounded by a powerful protective shield.
- My family, children, pets, and I are loved and safe.
- I surround my family with love and will not allow anyone to hurt them.
- My family and I are strong together, and we are each other's protective shields.
- My family is safe from psychic attacks.
- No one can hurt or influence my loved ones.
- My children and pets are always safe.
- A protective white light surrounds my children and keeps them safe.
- My loved ones are safe from (name person) harm.

- My loved ones are surrounded by a protective shield.
- A shield of light and love keeps my loved ones safe.

Salt Baths for Your Loved Ones

Protect your children and family members from psychic attacks by constantly encouraging them to take salt baths.

Ingredients:
- Salt
- Lavender
- Baking soda

Instructions:
1. Clean your bathtub thoroughly and declutter the bathroom creating a relaxing ambiance.
2. Add a few of their favorite items. If this bath is for your child, add their favorite toy.
3. You can add scented candles, protective crystals, plants, or diffuse essential oils; choose your favorite scents.
4. Play relaxing music.
5. Fill the bathtub with warm water, then add the salt, lavender, and baking soda.
6. Encourage them to take a bath for 20 to 30 minutes.

Protecting Someone from a Distance

You don't have to be in the same room with your children, pet, or family to shield them; you can protect them against psychic attacks from a distance.

Visualization Instructions:
1. Sit on a comfortable chair, close your eyes, and deeply breathe until you feel calm and relaxed.
2. Visualize your loved one surrounded by white protective light.
3. Focus on the image until you see it clearly.
4. Now, think of a happy memory you shared with them. Feel the joy you experienced together on that day, and let the positive vibes flow through you.

5.Spend a couple of minutes contemplating this feeling and your love for them.

6.Imagine these positive emotions have color, and imagine them leaving your body and entering the other person's protective shield.

7.Repeat, *"My loved one is protected by a powerful shield that only allows loving energy in."*

General Tips

- Be mindful of your energy so you can know when you are under psychic attacks.

- Focus on being emotionally stable and strong, so you won't be vulnerable to other people's negativity.

- Never hesitate to seek your guardian angel's or spiritual guide's help to protect you against psychic attacks.

- Whenever you think of the attacker, visualize showering them with pure white light while keeping your protective shield around you. No matter how tempting, never send them the same thoughts or energies they sent you. Remember, you are stronger than them, so meet their fear, hatred, jealousy, and anger with compassion, love, and understanding.

It isn't an exaggeration to say you are regularly under psychic attacks. Shield yourself and your loved ones every day to guarantee other people's darkness and negativity won't affect you. Treat the attacker with love and light. Don't stoop to their level or give in to anger or hatred. Although you can't control their actions, you are in control of your own reactions. Be the better person and return these attacks with positive energy, protecting you, and perhaps you can bring light into their dark world.

Incorporate these techniques into your daily routine. Even if you don't have time to meditate daily, memorize a few affirmations and repeat them when you wake up or on your way to work. Write them down on sticky notes and leave them in various places around the house, so your family can repeat them. Keep your thoughts positive and surround yourself and your loved ones with loving energy.

Chapter 10: Warding Rituals to Protect Your Home

Although shielding yourself and your loved ones against psychic attacks is essential, it won't be enough if your home isn't protected. Imagine you have the flu and taking medication but are constantly exposed to sick people. Will you ever recover? The same applies if you are surrounded by negativity; you will eventually catch these vibes. Your environment should be a sanctuary keeping you protected from psychic attacks.

This chapter covers various methods to shield your home, space, and altar from negative influences and entities.

Shielding your home is just as important as shielding yourself and your loved ones.
https://unsplash.com/photos/1ddol8rgUH8?utm_source=unsplash&utm_medium=referral&utm_content=creditShareLink

Warding Ritual

This ritual works for any physical space. It is a powerful technique to provide your home with permanent protection, so you only need to perform this ritual once in your life. Like a security system, it gives you control over what energies can enter your home and what you won't accept.

Ingredients and Tools:

- 4 jars with lids
- 4 metals or crystals associated with the archangel or deity you are summoning. For instance, if you are calling on the Archangel Gabriel, use aquamarine or citrine. If you summon Uriel, use tigers eye or amber.
- 4 crystals associated with your ancestor or spirit animal.
- 4 air crystals like fluorite, clear quartz, yellow topaz, yellow jasper, blue apatite, barite, or tanzanite
- 4 fire crystals like garnet, ruby, red jasper, carnelian, hematite, amber, sunstone, or pyrite.
- 4 water crystals like blue chalcedony, turquoise, chrysocolla, lapis lazuli, amethyst, chrysoprase, or moonstone
- 4 Earth crystals like emerald, green jade, moss agate, peridot, malachite, black obsidian, or black tourmaline
- 3 dried herbs of choice like lavender, rose petals, juniper, white sage, myrrh, frankincense, angelica root, bay, ginger, or cinnamon
- Pictures of your ancestors
- 1 black candle and 1 white candle
- 1 red tealight candle
- A bundle of purifying herbs like lavender, white sage, palo santo, and cedar
- 1 Bowl of purified water with sea salt

Instructions:

1. Declutter, clean, and organize your home, then purify it using a cleansing ritual.
2. Next, cleanse and shield your spirit.

3. Choose a quiet space with no distractions for your ritual, preferably an altar. Cleanse your altar before starting.

4. Place all the items on the altar to begin your ritual.

5. Sit in a comfortable position, close your eyes, and call on your guardian angel or spirit guide.

6. Set your intention. Say:

> *"I cleanse and protect my home from negative energies and influences. I ward my home so it becomes a safe haven of health, abundance, and peace. I will only allow love to enter my home."*

7. Light the black and white candles with the intention of banishing the negative influences. Leave them to burn out.

8. Light the herb bundle and the tealight candle. Put them on a heat-safe plate or bowl.

9. Open your front door, hold up the plate so the smoke floats outside the house, and say, "I bless and purify this home with fire and air." Then, draw a pentagram in the air using the smudge stick.

10. Visualize the negative energy blowing out of the door like smoke while repeating, "I bless this home with fire and air."

11. Move the burning herbs clockwise to purify the perimeter of your home. Cleanse the stairs, walls, floors, and every corner of the house. Draw a pentagram in the air near all openings like the fireplace, windows, doors, and mirrors.

12. When you have finished, return to the front door and repeat, "This house is protected by fire and air."

13. Take the bowl of salted water to the front door and repeat, "I bless my home with Earth and Water."

14. Dip your index finger in the water and draw a pentagram on the front door and the door's frame.

15. Visualize all the negativity leaving your home and going out of the front door.

16. Cleanse the perimeter of your home by walking around it clockwise, repeating, "I purify this home with Earth and water," and sprinkling water on the floor and every corner of the house.

17. Dip your finger in the water and draw a pentagram in the air over all the house's openings.

18. When you return to the front door, repeat this phrase: "This house is protected by Earth and water."

19. Return to your altar and repeat:

"I cleanse and protect my home from negative energies and influences. I ward my home so it becomes a safe haven of health, abundance, and peace. I will only allow love to enter my home."

20. Next, open your jars and put one air crystal, one fire crystal, one water crystal, one Earth crystal, 1 teaspoon of dry herbs, one crystal associated with the archangel you are summoning, and one stone associated with your ancestor or spirit animal in each.

21. Hold each ingredient, blow at it gently, tap it three times, and repeat "awake" to awaken its healing powers. Then repeat "(name the ingredient) strengthen the protective ward around my home." before you drop it in the jar.

22. Summon an archangel associated with the crystal before you put it in the jar, and tell him you seek his protective powers and make an offering in exchange for his help.

23. Write your ancestors' names on a piece of paper and place it near one of the jars with their photos.

24. Ask for their protection and ask them to keep your home safe.

25. You can make an offering to your ancestors, like their favorite drink, food, or flowers, to appease them.

26. Summon your ancestors the same way you summoned the archangel.

27. After placing all the ingredients in the jars, seal them tightly.

28. Hold each jar and repeat:

"This is a protective ward. May it guard the north side of my home and make it a safe haven of health, abundance, and peace. I will only allow love to enter my home."

29. Repeat the previous step with each jar and say the same intention mentioning a different direction each time (east, west, and south).

30. Tap on each jar with your index finger clockwise and repeat, "Safety, health, abundance, and peace."

31. Visualize an energy cone on top of each jar, feeding and nourishing it to protect your home.

32. Place one jar at the north corner of the house and the other three in the east, west, and south while visualizing threads coming out of each jar, making a big circle encompassing the whole house. (You can place the jars behind the furniture or bury them outdoors.)

33. Return to the altar, express your gratitude, and release all the energies and beings you summoned.

Herbs and Salt

Ingredients:
- 1 cup of sea salt
- ¼ cup of rosemary, raspberry, cinnamon, bay, pepper, and clove

Instructions:
1. Mix the ingredients together in a small bowl.
2. Place the bowl on your altar or at the door of the room you want to protect.

Salt Ritual

Ingredients and Tools:
- Pink Himalayan salt
- Dried bay leaves
- Dried rosemary
- Dried dill
- Cauldron or fire-proof bowl
- Pen and paper

Instructions:
1. Write the word "Protect" on a piece of paper and put it in the fire-proof bowl or cauldron.
2. Cover the piece of paper with the salt and dried herbs.

3. Place your hand over the bowl and visualize negative energy leaving your home and a large white circle enveloping it, shielding it from psychic attacks.

4. Next, burn the paper, salt, and herbs.

5. After they are burned down, wait for them to cool, then grind them into smaller pieces.

6. Put them in a glass jar, and place the jar anywhere in your home.

This ritual will keep your home safe for a whole year, so you can practice it once a year to protect your home from negative influences.

Practice Yoga

Yoga has always been an effective weapon against negativity since it reduces depression, stress, and anxiety. It has the same effect on physical spaces. Practice yoga in different spaces around the house, like near your altar or in a room you want to protect with the intention of shielding it from negative energy.

Full Moon Protection Ritual

The full moon symbolizes growth and protection. Protective rituals during this time are extremely powerful since lunar energy is a strong weapon against negativity.

Instructions:

1. During a full moon, find a quiet spot in your backyard, garden, or a room indoors with a window open so you can see the moon.

2. Cleanse the space using the white sage smudging ritual.

3. Next, sit comfortably, close your eyes, and take a few deep breaths.

4. Set an intention to protect your home against dark entities.

5. Meditate briefly and feel the moon's energy washing over you and your home.

6. Clear your thoughts and feel your body and mind relaxing.

7. Open your eyes and write on a piece of paper what you want to protect your home against. Repeat it out loud,

8. Hold a clear quartz crystal in your hand and close your eyes

9. Visualize the negativity leaving out the front door and the moon casting a huge protective bubble around your home.

10. Stay with this image for a few minutes. End the session by expressing your gratitude.

Herbs Ritual

Ingredients:

- Dried herbs like pepper, blueberry thrones, burdock root, bay leaves, basil leaves, cloves, and cinnamon.

Instructions:

1. Add all or some of the herbs into a small white pouch bag.

2. Set an intention with every herb, *"This herb will bless my home and shield it from psychic attacks."*

3. Tie the pouch bag with a black or red thread and repeat your intention.

4. Hang the bag on your front door.

Candle Ritual

You can use jar candles, tealight candles, or regular candles. However, jar candles are the best option.

Tools:

- 1 jar candle
- Dried herbs like lavender, basil, bay leaf, cinnamon, rosemary, and sage
- Marker

Instructions:

1. Cleanse the candle using a smudging ritual.

2. Write the word "Protect" on the candle's jar.

3. Light the candle and leave it for a few minutes.

4. Next, sprinkle the herbs over the candle while setting an intention like, *"I intend for these herbs to protect my home from negative influences."*

5. Leave the candle to burn for an hour, then blow it out.

6. Light it every day or every few days to keep your home safe.

Symbols Ritual

Instructions:

1. Draw a protective symbol like the eye of Horus, Hamsa Hand, mistletoe, pentacle, or another symbol on a candle's jar.

2. Light the candle and sit in front of it, staring at the flame.

3. Visualize a protective circle coming out of the flame surrounding your home and shielding it from psychic attacks.

Runes Rituals

Runes are the alphabet in Norse mythology. It comprises twenty-four letters, and all have divine powers.

Tools:

- Flat stone
- Illustrations of protective runes like Algiz, Tiwaz, Ehwaz, Eihwaz, Ingwaz, and Thurisaz

Instructions:

1. Sit in a quiet room and take a few minutes to clear your head.

2. Carve the runes on the flat stone while remaining focused and present in the moment.

3. Set an intention for these runes to fulfill their purpose and protect your home.

4. When you're finished carving, run your hands over the runes while thinking of protecting your home.

5. Choose the rune you feel is powerful enough to shield your home and defend it against psychic attacks. Follow your gut since the right rune will call you.

6. Once you find it, study its shape.

7. Sit comfortably, close your eyes, and take a few deep breaths.

8. Visualize the rune casting a white protective light around your home.

9. Sit with this image for a while.

10. You can also carve the rune on coins and hang them on your front door or elsewhere around the house.

Trataka Meditation

Trataka is an ancient meditation technique usually practiced during a yoga session. It involves intense gazing, focus, and being present in the moment.

Instructions:

1. Place a candle on the floor and light it.

2. Sit in a comfortable position opposite the candle.

3. Gaze at it for three minutes without blinking; you can set a timer beforehand.

4. Expect your eyes to tear up.

5. After three minutes, close your eyes, and the image of the candle's flame will appear to you.

6. Sit with this image for a while until it goes away.

7. Open your eyes and stare at the void between any two objects in the room.

8. This void represents the negativity inside your home.

9. Close your eyes and visualize this void shrinking and disappearing for good.

Crystals Ritual

Tools: Four black tourmaline (or any black crystals

Instructions:

1. You should practice grounding meditation first for this ritual to work.

2. Sit in a comfortable position and close your eyes.

3. Inhale and exhale deeply, focusing on your breath and your chest's movement.

4. Visualize a white light from above entering your body through your ground chakra.

5. Imagine the light moving down your spine, leaving through your feet, and disappearing into the Earth.

6. Feel the negativity inside your body moving down your spine, exiting through your feet, and disappearing into the Earth.

7. Next, visualize pure white light from the Earth entering your body through your feet.

8. Feel the Earth's protection washing over you and repeat, "I connect with Mother Earth, and she covers me with her protection."

9. End this session by expressing gratitude to Mother Earth, then open your eyes.

10. You are now ready to practice the crystals ritual.

11. Hold the four black crystals and raise them to the area between your eyebrows (your third eye chakra).

12. Set your intention whether you want to protect your home, specific room, or your altar. Say, *"I program this crystal to protect my space from negative energy."*

13. Place each of the crystals in a different corner around the house. Ensure you place one at the front door to shield your home from negative influences.

Onion Braid

Ingredients:

- Onions with green tops
- 4 feet of twine

Instructions:

1. Fold the twine in half, then tie a knot at its end to create a loop.

2. Put the twine on a flat surface and place an onion upside down. The green tops should form a third string next to the twine's two free ends.

3. Make a tight braid with the three strings.

4. Next, braid the rest of the onions with the twine, focusing on your intention. Say, *"I am making this charm to protect my home and keep negative energy at bay."*

5. Hang them on your front door or on the wall of the room you want to protect.

Charm Ritual

Ingredients:

- Rosemary or yarrow
- 1 protective crystal like malachite, black tourmaline, or smoky quartz
- 1 protective symbol, like crossed spears or Hamsa Hand
- A small bag, preferably black

Instructions:

1. Practice grounding meditation before you perform this ritual.
2. Next, place each item in the bag while visualizing a protective white light emitting from them, creating a protective bubble surrounding your home. The bubble only allows positive and loving energies in and keeps the darkness and negativity at bay.
3. After you put all the items in the bag, place your hand on it. Repeat the Kundalini protection mantra:

   Aad Guray Nameh, *"I call upon the primal wisdom, I bow to the truth that has existed for ages, I summon the true wisdom, I bow to the Divine wisdom."*

4. Keep repeating the mantra until you sense the energy shifting.
5. Place the bag in the room you want to protect.

Pray to the Four Elements

Instructions:

1. Sit in a comfortable position and take a few deep breaths.
2. Once you feel centered and calm, repeat this chant three times:

   "Elements of the day and elements of the sun, I beseech you to come my way. I summon the powers of the day and night, and I pray you protect my home."

3. Close your eyes and visualize a golden ball of energy surrounding your home, growing bigger and stronger each time you chant.

Affirmations

- My home is protected and guarded.
- My home keeps me safe and secure.

- No unwanted energy can get into my home.
- Only love and light can enter my home.
- The universe places a shield around my home.
- Positive vibrations surround my space.
- My home is protecting me.
- The universe prevents negativity from entering my home.
- I am releasing all unwanted energy from my home.
- Positivity and love emit from my home.
- I prevent negative energy from entering my space.
- The universe is making my home a safe haven.
- No negativity is allowed in my home.
- A strong protective field envelops my home; nothing can get in.
- All negative influences are released from my home.
- There is no room in my space for fear and anxiety.
- Only positive vibes are welcomed in my home.
- My space emits positivity and peace.
- My space is protected from bad vibes.
- My home protects my energy.
- My loved ones are safe in my home.
- I am grateful for the positive energy shielding my space.
- Divine protection keeps my home safe.
- My home is a magnet, only attracting love and positivity.
- I am protected from negative influences.
- I am grateful for the divine's protection.
- I choose to feel safe in my space.
- Bad energy can't penetrate my home's shield.
- I am safe in my surroundings.
- Nothing bad can happen. My space keeps me safe.
- I welcome the universe's protection.
- My home vibrates positive energy.
- I am not afraid. I feel secure in my environment.
- I am cleansing my space of negative influences.

- My home is my boundary; it keeps me safe.
- I release the negativity from my home to free space for love and abundance.
- Nothing can get into my house without my permission.
- My home only welcomes positive energy.
- Protective energy guards my space.
- Positivity and wisdom surround my space.
- My home is free of negative energies.
- My guardian angel is watching over my space.

Negative influences can easily find their way into your home. Practice any of these rituals whenever you feel a shift in energy or bad vibes is taking over your space. Always protect your home by placing protective symbols, crystals, herbs, or an onion braid around your home.

Conclusion

You've reached the end of this book and are significantly more informed about your psychic energy and those around you, particularly negative energies and attacks. Even when you're confident of being in a positive space and energy, negativity can attack, *but now you know how to deal with it.*

Psychic attacks can significantly impact your mood and mental and physical health. They can lower your home's vibration and spread negativity to every aspect of your life. Avoiding negative energy isn't realistic since people and objects carry bad vibes influencing you daily. However, practicing certain cleansing rituals and spiritual work can shield you from negativity and low vibrations.

The book began by explaining the concept of psychic attacks and negative energy. It provided exercises so you could better understand how energy works, and then we discussed psychic protection and its many benefits.

You can't protect yourself against psychic attacks without raising your vibration and sharpening your psychic skills first. The second chapter provided multiple instructions and tips, including breathing exercises, meditation, and visualization techniques to prepare your psyche for protection. Your soul and karma also require cleansing to clear past energies and influences so you are ready to receive positive energy. The book included effective techniques to purify your soul and discussed the concept of karma, how external influences alter it, and what you can do to protect yourself.

Negative energy can impact your home, pets, and family. The book discussed how to identify negative energy in your home and provided multiple cleansing rituals you can perform to cleanse your space and loved ones.

The word "aura" is often mentioned during discussions of the psyche and spiritual work. The book explains this concept in detail and its connection to the soul. Negative energy is powerful enough to damage your aura. The book discussed identifying when it is damaged and various healing techniques. It explained the significance of a strong aura against psychic attacks.

Every person has a guardian angel helping, protecting, and guiding them. The book explains the role of these angels in your life and how you can summon them to defend yourself or a loved one against psychic attacks.

After providing all the information to prepare yourself for protection, the book's second part focuses on self-defense against psychic attacks, introducing symbols, plants, crystals, and their protective purposes. Then, it focused on curses, hexes, and unwanted attachments by defining each concept and how to recognize if you are a victim. It covered multiple rituals and methods to break these spells.

You are constantly exposed to psychic attacks wherever you go, but if you can protect yourself against these influences, you can keep yourself and your loved ones safe. The last part of the book focused on protection techniques to use on yourself, your family, and your pets. It provided warding rituals to protect your home, space, and altar.

Let this book guide you and use all the rituals, tips, and techniques mentioned to shield yourself and everything you hold dear from psychic attacks.

Part 2: Kundalini Yoga

Secrets to Unlocking Energy, Cleansing Chakras, and Awakening the Shakti within with Kriya

Introduction

Have you ever felt the urge to take a deep dive into the mysticism of your being? Kundalini yoga is one way you can do this. It is an ancient spiritual practice that will awaken the dormant energy within your body.

Kundalini yoga is an effective method for connecting with the three elements that make us human, our physical, mental, and spiritual health. Through various meditation tools, breathwork, mudras, mantras, and asanas (yoga poses), the practice focuses on unlocking our potential to open the energy of the seven chakras in the body. Increasing awareness of these channels shows us how to explore the connection between body and mind in our daily lives.

Self-care is vital to a healthy state of mind, body, and spirit. A critical element in caring for ourselves is learning to balance the chakras, the energy centers of our being. As we take time to nurture each one through practices such as yoga, meditation, or visualization, we discover new reserves of self-love. We come to understand that by focusing on inner peace, we can learn to prioritize our holistic health, be kind to ourselves and form healthier connections with the outside world.

Our spirit's journey consists of more than simply our physical body. It is also connected to ethereal energies found in the seven chakras along the spine. We can restore balance in our lives by gaining insight into each one and how it relates to others. Learning about the associated colors, emotions, and mental states related to each chakra helps us become more aware of them so that better alignment can be attained. Understanding how they relate allows us to travel a smoother pathway toward true spiritual enlightenment.

When the Kundalini energy is awakened, it brings awareness of our inner power. A surge of energy is activated, allowing us to reach our full potential and experience a fuller sense of life force. We become more conscious of our physical and spiritual selves, improving our sense of clarity and inner calm. We can then channel this heightened energy into a more focused and conscious state of being.

Regardless of which stage of the Kundalini journey you are at, this book will guide you through this mystical and magical journey. It will take you through the steps of beginning your Kundalini yoga practice. It will explain what to expect, how to prepare, and give tips on maintaining the energy flow for a successful journey. As we go through each chapter, take your time, and explore the depths of your spiritual being. Acknowledge your inner wisdom and use it to guide you. This is an exciting time for personal growth. May your journey be filled with love, light, and peace. Namaste!

Chapter 1: You and Your Kundalini Shakti

Ancient Eastern philosophy has long taught the concept of shakti and Kundalini, a spiritual force complemented by yogic practice. Although these concepts date back centuries, they are becoming increasingly popular in modern-day self-improvement. Through guided meditation and physical exercise, yoga adherents often report mastering a sixth sense and an ability to connect with their inner energy –once solely the domain of spiritual gurus and psychics. Shakti and Kundalini allow those on the journey to enlightenment to reach higher levels of focus, truth, and power within themselves. As such, it is clear why these two ancient concepts remain popular today.

Shakti is a form of divine energy. This is the Hindu depiction of Shakti.

This chapter will introduce you to the concept of shakti and Kundalini as it is found in different traditions worldwide. We will first explain the connection between shakti and Kundalini, then explore how they are expressed in various religions, such as Buddhism, Hinduism, Christianity, and even Kabbalistic mysticism or Jungian psychology. Next, we will explore the many benefits of practicing this type of yoga, including physical, mental, and spiritual well-being. This chapter will then go on to discuss what happens when Kundalini is awakened, as well as provide a few real-life accounts. This chapter will also go through each of the four stages of Kundalini awakening and answer any frequently asked questions about it. By the end of this chapter, you'll have a thorough understanding of what shakti and Kundalini are all about.

Introduction to Shakti and Kundalini

Shakti and Kundalini are concepts most often associated with Hinduism and other similar spiritual belief systems. Shakti is a form of divine energy believed to be the source of all creation and enlightenment, while Kundalini is a sleeping coiled energy at the base of each person's spine that must be awakened to reach the highest states of spiritual attainment. Through meditation, movements such as yoga, spiritual practice, and devotion, one can access this powerful energy, which opens the door to unleashing their deeper potential to work towards enlightenment. Once awakened, releasing this power can bring joy, understanding, connection, and direct experience with our true selves.

Shakti, originating from the Hindu tradition, is a feminine divine energy bestowed on all living things at the time of creation. It is often symbolized by different goddesses like Kali and Durga and is believed to bring change into the universe. Shakti radiates power, courage, and willpower associated with motherhood and nurturing qualities. Its cosmic power is transferred through intricate yogic practices and spiritual journeys. Shakti's close connection to Kundalini energy is grounded in its capacity to awaken an individual's internal energy and transform it into powerful energy toward personal enlightenment. Historically, shakti was seen as a way to gain control over one's inner strength. This feeds into the larger societal search for balance between female dominance (grace and compassion) alongside male dominance (physical strength).

The Different Traditions of Kundalini

While sourced from a common set of teachings, several different branches of Kundalini traditions have evolved. From the Sikh tradition in India and its Los Angeles-based offshoot to modern interpretations, this form of spiritual practice has continued to expand and become more accessible worldwide. Each iteration empowers practitioners with unique methods for unlocking their path to higher consciousness, allowing them to explore various aspects of this exciting and rewarding spiritual journey.

A. Buddhism

Founded more than 2,500 years ago in India, the Buddhist tradition contains within it a multifaceted practice of energizing the body and mind. One such practice is that of Kundalini, an ancient meditation discipline focusing on understanding and activating energy stored in the lower spine. By concentrating on energy flows and visualization, practitioners can align their bodies and minds to be open to higher spiritual insights and practical, emotional healing. Kundalini practices have been popular in India for a long time, but they have recently gained popularity in western countries due to advances in yoga science and spiritual studies. It offers an excellent way for people to access the deeper truths of their being, creating a safe place to explore the power of their consciousness.

B. Hinduism

Hinduism is famously known for its wide variety of traditions and rituals, including the Kundalini. This yogic practice is a spiritual rite that works to awaken energy in the body and provide it with heightened awareness and consciousness. It is known that achieving the desired level of Kundalini can lead to greater knowledge and enlightenment. Since believed to be a connection between physical and non-physical energies, it is said that when trained correctly, a person can experience an intense realization of their inner soul. Thus, Kundalini is an essential part of Hindu tradition as it empowers one to open up more dimensions within themselves, ultimately furthering our understanding of spirituality.

C. Christianity

Christianity is an ancient faith that incorporates a multitude of traditions, ranging from a code of ethics to communion and healing. One of the most interesting aspects of Christianity is the tradition of Kundalini, an energetic force associated with the seven chakras, or points of spiritual energy located along the spine. Christian writers have interpreted this as God's living Spirit touching believers through grace. Contemplative practices such as Lectio Divina incorporate Christian principles alongside Kundalini in specifically designed breathing techniques to create powerful experiences for many followers of Christ. Thus, Kundalini is often interwoven into one's practice within modern Christianity as a way to access spiritual awakening and connection with God.

D. Kabbalistic Mysticism

Kabbalistic Mysticism has been practiced for centuries and is based on ancient Jewish mysticism. Its teachings revolve around the idea of using esoteric knowledge and techniques to connect with divinity. The Kundalini tradition is a part of this practice which involves awakening spiritual energies found within every human being to increase self-awareness and potentially reveal the secrets of the universe. It's considered to be a spiritual journey that leads individuals to deeper levels of understanding and connection with something greater than themselves, often through meditative practices such as yoga postures or chanting mantras. The goal of Kabbalistic Mysticism and the tradition of Kundalini are quite different from those associated with other religions. Still, it provides practitioners with a powerful window into the innermost core of their existence, allowing them to experience life on a deeper level.

E. Jungian Psychology

Jungian psychology offers us a unique way of understanding our inner workings through the traditions of Kundalini. This belief is based on the idea of an energy system within the human body, composed of seven major chakras or spiritual power points that work together to bring about wholeness. According to Jungian thought, this energy is activated through an *initiatory experience*, an event or process that forces or allows for a fundamental change in one's life and identity. By engaging with this powerful energy, we can begin to explore ideas like transformation, self-actualization, and reintegration with the unconscious psyche. Through its tradition of utilizing Kundalini, Jungian psychology allows us a more holistic approach to understanding our psyches and working towards wholeness.

Kundalini Yoga

Kundalini Yoga is an ancient practice for spiritual development and self-transformation, using specific kriyas and asanas to help you access your cosmic consciousness. This powerful practice involves connecting with the energy stored within you and in universal consciousness, known as Kundalini. Through focused breathing, meditation, chanting, and other exercises, practitioners of Kundalini Yoga can tap into this powerful force in ways that create physical, mental, and spiritual change.

Kriyas are sets of postures synchronized with the breath to raise or release vital energies, working on the nervous and glandular systems within the body. Asanas are postures designed to increase strength and flexibility while calming the nervous system. Discovering this potent form of yoga will help anyone who integrates its teachings into their daily life experience greater alignment with their true nature.

The Benefits of Kundalini Yoga

With its focus on harnessing the energy and channeling it through poses, breathing techniques, and meditation, Kundalini imparts a range of physical, mental, and spiritual benefits to dedicated practitioners. Physically, Kundalini yoga can improve flexibility, reduce stress, boost metabolism, and increase endurance. On a mental level, it improves concentration, reduces anxiety and depression, and even lifts moods. Those who work with Kundalini have also reported spiritual growth, such as higher states of consciousness, enhanced creativity, and a deep reconnection with their true selves. All these rewards make this traditional practice well worth looking into for anybody looking to deepen their yoga practice or break free from the stresses of modern life.

A. Physical Benefits

One of the major positive spinoffs of Kundalini yoga is stress relief. It's a wonderful way to reduce tension and help restore balance in your body and mind. Kundalini yoga is particularly useful due to its focus on deep breaths and slow, gentle postures/exercises that activate the energy centers throughout the body. This keeps the energy flowing smoothly, reducing stress while increasing flexibility. Over time, regular practice really can change how you feel by improving your energy level overall. With increased flexibility stemming from the physical involvement in the poses and exercises, higher energy levels as a result of improved breathing habits, and reduced stress thanks to targeted breathing techniques, there are many rewards to be gained through Kundalini yoga for those looking for an effective way to cultivate their strength and well-being.

B. Mental Benefits

Practicing Kundalini yoga has several mental benefits, such as promoting clarity of mind, enhancing self-awareness, and improving concentration. Clarity of mind is found through meditative practices like Kundalini Yoga which help by slowing down the mind's inner chatter. Regular practice reduces feelings of anxiety and stress, replacing them with a more peaceful mindset. Increased self-awareness can help us explore past traumas and easily identify dysfunctional habits. Kundalini's powerful healing mantras can open us up to experience new levels within ourselves we didn't know existed. Lastly, practicing Kundalini Yoga, with its combination of dynamic breathing techniques and vigorous movement, can naturally improve concentration levels without any external tools like medication or supplements. Overall, it's no secret why so many people turn to this form of yoga, as an abundance of mental health-related benefits is associated with it.

C. Spiritual Benefits

Kundalini yoga provides spiritual benefits such as connecting with the divine, gaining wisdom, and accessing higher states of consciousness. When practicing Kundalini yoga, you open yourself up to the divine. You create an inner connection that can be used to explore your beliefs and spirituality. You'll also gain spiritual wisdom while practicing this ancient form of yoga, awakening you to a greater understanding of yourself and life. Finally, Kundalini Yoga can open access to higher states of consciousness that you may not have felt before. It is perfect for those seeking enlightenment or seeking to expand awareness and uncover greater depths within themselves.

Kundalini Awakening: What Happens When It Is Awakened

Kundalini awakening is a complex process that can open up the powerful spiritual life force within. This awakening process can bring physical, emotional, mental, and spiritual transformation. Some of the signs associated with this process are increased intuition, enhanced healing abilities, and improved creativity and focus. Furthermore, Kundalini Awakening can open up spiritual passages to higher levels of consciousness. It has been known to cause the direct experience of psychic powers, clairvoyance, deep insight into your true path in life, and absolute understanding of the cosmic laws of nature. All these possible outcomes make Kundalini Awakening a journey worth taking.

Real-Life Accounts of Kundalini Awakening

Kundalini Awakening, also known as *pranotthana* or *spiritual enlightenment,* is a phenomenon that has been described by many as a life-changing experience. While many people look to religious texts and ancient traditions to understand this state of being, anyone curious about it can find real-life accounts of the event all over the internet. Through interviews, personal journeys, and journal entries, we can see how people came in contact with this spiritual energy and how it changed their lives. Experiences vary from moments of incredible joy and peace right through to an almost overwhelming force that proves difficult to handle. To understand this special moment, nothing replaces hearing stories first-hand from those who went through an authentic Kundalini awakening themselves. Here are some of the most inspiring and enlightening accounts of Kundalini awakenings that we have found:

A. The Awakening of Purna

Purna was a student of yoga who had been studying and practicing for many years. One day she was meditating and felt a sudden surge of energy that was so powerful she wasn't sure if it was an inner experience or something external. She soon realized that this was the awakening of her Kundalini energy. This event transformed Purna into a more intuitive, sensitive, and calm person. She felt connected on a much deeper level with her body, mind, and spirit. Her physical health improved, too, as she no longer suffered from the back pain that had plagued her for years.

B. The Divine Light of David

David was a spiritual seeker who wanted to experience a connection with the divine. As he was meditating one day, he suddenly felt a light enter his body. He said it was like a force of energy that filled him with love, peace, and joy. He experienced a state of clarity and understanding that he had never known before. He described the feeling as an immense power, unlike anything he had ever felt.

C. The Higher Consciousness of Mariel

Mariel was a student of yoga and meditation. She was on a quest to find her true purpose in life when she experienced a powerful Kundalini awakening. She felt an energy that filled her with a deep understanding and connection to the universe. She had what she described as a "profound spiritual revelation," which allowed her to see beyond the physical realm and understand the interconnectedness of all things. Through this experience, Mariel gained a sense of deeper meaning in her life and a greater connection to the spiritual world.

These are just a few of the many real-life accounts out there. While each story is very personal, they all have one thing in common: they illustrate a powerful insight into the potential of Kundalini awakening and the positive transformation it can bring. If you feel called to explore this phenomenon further, many resources are out there to help you on your journey. Don't hesitate to take the leap and explore what spiritual enlightenment can bring to your life.

The Four Stages of Kundalini Awakening

Kundalini awakening consists of a journey of four distinct stages: awakening, cleansing, absorption, and the final stage. During the Awakening stage (Arambha), the spiritual seeker can raise their frequency level to contact their higher self. In the Cleansing stage (Ghata), one goes through processes such as negative feelings, thought patterns, and outmoded beliefs that may be blocking you from connecting more deeply with yourself.

Once this is done, you are ready to move into the Absorption stage (*Pacihaya*), where you can become fully aware of your higher self and manifest your true desires. Lastly, in the Final stage (Nishpatti), the integration of all aspects of self fully leads one to complete illumination and enlightenment. The practice of Kundalini awakening is a powerful tool for those who seek inner peace and transformation.

While the process can be challenging, the rewards are great. Those who embark on this path will find themselves changed profoundly and with a greater sense of connection to their higher self. Regardless of which stage you are at in your spiritual journey, Kundalini awakening can be a powerful tool to help you reach the next level.

FAQs

While Kundalini awakenings can be a deeply spiritual and personal experience, many people have questions about the process. Here are some of the most common FAQs about Kundalini awakenings and the stages of spiritual transformation.

Q: Is It Dangerous?

A: Kundalini awakenings are not in and of themselves dangerous. However, it is crucial to be mindful of the intensity of the energy as it can be overwhelming and potentially negatively impacts one's physical, mental, and emotional health. Working with an experienced teacher or practitioner who can support and guide you through the process is essential.

Q: Is Kundalini Awakening Difficult?

A: Every Kundalini awakening is unique and can vary in difficulty. It depends on the individual's level of spiritual practice, emotional and physical health, and comfort level with the process. It is a transformative journey and requires patience, practice, and dedication. You should work with a teacher or practitioner who can provide guidance and support.

Q: How Long Does the Process Take?

A: Kundalini awakenings can take anywhere from a few weeks to several years. It is essential to be patient and to trust in the process. By working alongside a certified teacher or practitioner, you can ensure your journey is safe and successful. It is also crucial to be mindful of one's emotional and physical well-being to ensure the journey is healthy and beneficial.

Q: Can Anyone Awaken Their Kundalini?

A: Kundalini awakenings are available to all individuals who are willing to embark on the journey. It is crucial, however, to be mindful of one's physical, mental, and emotional health before beginning the process. You should also work with an experienced teacher or practitioner who can provide guidance and support throughout the process.

Q. Is It Worth Pursuing?

A: If you seek a spiritual path of greater inner knowledge and connection to the divine, then Kundalini awakening can be incredibly rewarding. It can bring intense clarity, greater purpose, and a profound sense of knowing. With patience and dedication, the process can offer tremendous insight and transformation that can be deeply meaningful and beneficial.

Kundalini awakening is a powerful opportunity for spiritual transformation, self-discovery, and connection with the divine. It is an ancient practice used for centuries to help seekers gain inner knowledge, peace, and transformation. By understanding the stages of spiritual transformation, the potential risks and benefits of Kundalini awakenings, and the importance of working with an experienced teacher, you can ensure that your journey is safe and successful.

Chapter 2: Get to Know Your Chakras

Kundalini awakening is an ancient yogic practice that countless masters have tapped into over the centuries. It is essentially a way to unleash the hidden, untapped potential within each of us. Kundalini awakening first requires settling and calming the mind so that our inner force can be revealed in its purest form. Once we connect with our Kundalini (also known as life force energy), we open ourselves up to heightened consciousness and spiritual transformations. This allows us to experience higher levels of awareness and perception than ever before.

In unlocking the dormant power available via Kundalini, we connect with ourselves on an entirely new level. It is a sacred practice that has existed since the dawn of time. The chakras play a pivotal role in the Kundalini process, as they are the energy centers that the awakened energy will "slither" through on its journey up the spine. This chapter will act as a general presentation of the chakras and their connection with the Kundalini energy. It will illustrate the chakra's symbol, Sanskrit name, and its location and role in the system. It will cover each chakra's color, sound, and mantra. We'll also explore blockage symptoms and clear chakra sensations which can be experienced when the chakras are open.

Introduction to the Chakras

The chakras are ancient Indian energy centers that have long been associated with physical, mental, and spiritual well-being. Each of the seven main chakras located along the spine corresponds to different states of consciousness and is believed to influence how we take in the process and express life's energy. To help balance our energetic system, we can use various tools such as affirmations, breathing techniques, visualizations, sound healing, and yoga to open the flow of energy through each chakra and awaken a more mindful connection with our inner selves. Understanding how these powerful energy centers interact with us in unique ways and how we can facilitate their natural flow of life force will help us ultimately achieve our highest potential.

Muladhara: The Root Chakra

The Muladhara, the root chakra, serves as the foundation of the human body's energy system. This base-level energetic center helps fuel our physical and emotional well-being by drawing energy from the earth and providing a power source for our lives. The associated element to this chakra is earth, so grounding ourselves is key for keeping this chakra balanced and active. When feeling ungrounded or disrupted in balance, one can reconnect with their root chakra through activities such as yoga, dancing, or meditating outdoors or on the ground. This allows us to remain centered and at peace within our skin.

The root chakra.
https://pixabay.com/es/illustrations/chakra-mandala-chakra-ra%c3%adz-1340058/

A. Symbol and Sanskrit Name

The symbol associated with the root chakra is a four-petaled lotus flower that sits atop a square. The Sanskrit name for this chakra is Muladhara, which translates to "root support" or "base."

B. Location and Role

Muladhara can be found at the base of the spine. It is associated with safety, security, and stability. It is a grounding chakra, which means that it keeps us connected with reality and allows us to have balanced physical energy. Emotionally, Muladhara provides us with feelings of security and trust in ourselves and our environment. Physically, this chakra's balanced energy gives us good posture, strong immunity, and balanced metabolism. Activating this energy center also makes it easier for people to manifest their desires as it increases their ability to stay focused on their goals.

C. Color, Sound, and Mantra

The Muladhara is the foundation for the entire energetic system in the body. Represented by a deep red color and a steady drumbeat, its energy is focused on feeling secure and grounded in our environment. The root chakra can be aligned with meditation involving mantras repeated silently to oneself, such as "I am safe." This mantra helps to open and balance the energetic state of mind allowing for higher levels of well-being.

D. Blockage Symptoms

When we experience a blockage to this chakra, it can manifest in many physical, mental, and emotional symptoms. Low energy, insecurity, feeling disconnected from others, and difficulty grounding yourself are some common signs of imbalance. Digestive problems or accidents can indicate that our root chakra needs attention and should not be ignored. Clearing out any stagnant energy from this chakra will restore balance to your overall well-being and make you feel secure.

E. Clear Chakra Sensations

When experiencing a clear Muladhara, you may feel lighter in your body, as if the weight on your shoulders has been lifted. You may also feel more grounded and connected to the earth, with a strong sense of stability and security. Physically, your digestive system might work better, releasing stagnant energy and helping you digest food more effectively. Mentally, a clear root chakra can help you feel less stressed and overwhelmed by everyday life. Furthermore, a balanced root chakra helps us accept our intuition and have faith in the unknown. All these effects result from unlocking an open chakra, which allows us to tap into inner strength and connect with our true selves.

Svadhisthana: The Sacral Chakra

The Sacral Chakra is associated with emotion and creativity and helps to process our physical and emotional experiences. This chakra regulates our feelings of pleasure, sensuality, and relationships with ourselves and others. When this chakra is balanced, we can relate to life from a place of joy instead of fear or guilt. Free-flowing energy in this area allows us to let go of expectations or self-judgment, enabling us to move joyfully through life's challenges and accept what it offers us. Practicing yoga poses that focus on alignment, breath work, and grounding activities (like journaling) can help restore harmony in the sacral chakra so we can experience life with an open heart.

The sacral chakra.

A. Symbol and Sanskrit Name

The *Svadhisthana* in Sanskrit, or "sacral chakra, is located on the pelvic floor and is represented by a lotus flower with six orange petals. This chakra's energy controls creativity, relationships, sex drive, and emotions such as pleasure and sensuality. It encourages you to accept and explore yourself and your passions without judgment. Harnessing this chakra's power has many proven health benefits, including improved mental clarity and emotional balance.

B. Location and Role

Svadhisthana, one of the seven primary chakras associated with Hindu and Buddhist practices, is also known as the sacral chakra. It is located below the naval, just above the pelvic area. It is mostly connected to relationships and sexuality. However, it can be used in so much more. Svadhisthana is known to bring creativity and joy when opened up properly. People can use its powers for emotional intelligence, healing from trauma, and connecting with physical sensibilities (taste, smell, touch). To tap into this positivity, one must learn to meditate on this energetic center to open themselves up emotionally and be mindful of their decisions. Then they can truly benefit from Svadhishthana's wisdom.

C. Color, Sound, and Mantra

Svadhisthana is associated with the color orange, the sound "Vam," and the mantra "I Feel." Svadhisthana represents our emotional life and sexual energy. Working with this chakra allows us to tap into our creativity, express ourselves more freely, and access greater spiritual abundance. Embracing our creative potential encourages us to take risks and find the courage within. Inviting in the orange hue of Svadhisthana supports feelings of pleasure and flow as we work towards living authentically!

D. Blockage Symptoms

When this chakra is blocked or imbalanced, we may experience a feeling of disconnection with our bodies or emotions. Along with physical sensations such as pain in the groin or lower back area, you may feel insecure or lack trust in yourself or others. You may also have difficulty relating to relationships on an emotional level. Low energy levels, feelings of being stuck in life, and general apathy towards activities that would normally be enjoyable could be signs that you have a blockage in your Svadhisthana chakra.

E. Clear Chakra Sensations

When this chakra is balanced, we feel free from emotion's grip as our body fills with pleasurable sensations. On the other hand, when it is blocked or unbalanced, we experience negative emotions such as jealousy and insecurity that arise in our inner waters. Opening this chakra allows us to explore our creative side without fear and increase pleasure through natural expression. Achieving balance starts with becoming aware of your feelings and understanding yourself. Regular exercise and yoga can help you clear pathways and open up energy flow to create a state of harmony.

Manipura: The Solar Plexus Chakra

Manipura, or the solar plexus chakra, is one of seven chakras in the human body and is associated with self-empowerment and purpose. Many spiritualists believe that it is the core center of willpower and strength. Tapping into Manipura serves as a turbo boost for our mental and physical vitality. Working on this chakra can help us approach life with enthusiasm, drive, clarity, and confidence. Meditation allows us to access these powerful qualities within ourselves; drawing out the unique energy found in Manipura with each breath can be particularly effective. As we commit to unblocking our solar plexus chakra, we make progress toward unlocking our true potential!

The solar plexus chakra.
https://pixabay.com/es/illustrations/mandala-chakra-del-plexo-solar-1340066/

A. Symbol and Sanskrit Name

Manipura is represented by a downward-pointing triangle, symbolizing our innate power and the fire from within. Its Sanskrit name means "lustrous gem;" it is located in the solar plexus.

B. Role and Benefits

Manipura serves as a great source of power in our lives. It is the gateway to manifesting our dreams and aspirations through action. When its energy is balanced, we experience an increase in self-confidence, a greater ability to make decisions and feel empowered. We can also enhance our physical energy, strengthen our digestion, and increase our ability to take on challenging tasks.

C. Color, Sound, and Mantra

Manipura is associated with the color yellow and the sound "Ram." Its mantra is "I Do." Working with the vibration of this chakra can help us move forward in our lives and take control of our destinies.

D. Blockage Symptoms

When this chakra is blocked or out of balance, we tend to feel emotionally and physically sluggish. Low levels of energy, difficulty making decisions, feelings of insecurity, and an inability to take risks are all signs that work is needed to clear blockages in your Manipura chakra. Other common physical symptoms of a blocked Manipura include digestive issues, fatigue, and aches in the upper body.

E. Clear Chakra Sensations

When Manipura is balanced, we experience a surge of energy that allows us to move through life with direction and purpose. We can confidently make decisions, trust our intuition, and leap into unknown territory. To open this chakra, practice yoga and meditate on working with its mantra "I Do." Feel empowered and free as you unlock the potential of your solar plexus chakra!

Anahata: The Heart Chakra

The Anahata, or heart chakra, is one of the seven primary chakras of the human energy system. It relates to matters of compassion, love, and emotional balance in our lives. Through building this chakra's energy, we can learn to integrate these qualities into our lives as tools for personal growth. Working with the Anahata implies being in touch with all other chakras and understanding their relationship to create a healthy state of being. Therapeutic practices such as meditation and yoga are among the suggested forms of developing Anahata's energy, offering insight into how to access more heartfelt emotions. With mindfulness practices related to this energy center, we cultivate inner peace and feelings of unconditional love for both ourselves and others.

The heart chakra.

A. Symbol and Sanskrit Name

Anahata is represented by a lotus flower with twelve petals, signifying its connection to the heart. Its Sanskrit name means "unhurt" and is in the center of the chest.

B. Role and Benefits

Anahata bridges our physical and spiritual bodies, allowing us to connect with our higher self. When its energy is balanced, we experience increased compassion, self-love, and the ability to forgive and accept. We can also enhance our creativity and emotional intelligence, increase our capacity for empathy, and build strong relationships.

C. Color, Sound, and Mantra

Anahata is associated with the color green and the sound "Yam." Its mantra is "I Love." Working with this chakra vibration can help us open our hearts and cultivate feelings of love, acceptance, and compassion.

D. Blockage Symptoms

When this chakra is blocked or out of balance, we tend to feel emotionally disconnected from others and find it hard to trust in relationships. Feelings of loneliness, fear of intimacy, and difficulty expressing emotions are all signs that you may need to work on clearing some blockages in your Anahata chakra. Other common physical symptoms of a blocked Anahata include heart palpitations, chest pain, and immune system issues.

E. Clear Chakra Sensations

When Anahata is balanced, we experience a sense of inner peace and contentment. We can accept our own emotions, as well as those of others, without judgment or fear. To open this chakra, practice yoga and meditation on working with its mantra, "I Love." Feel the love that radiates from your heart, the unconditional love you have for yourself and others!

Vishuddha: The Throat Chakra

The throat chakra is one of seven major energy centers within the body, known as Vishuddha. Its relevance and importance lie in its ability to open our vocal cords and express truth and creativity. With energy flowing freely through this chakra, we can harness our power of communication. This can improve our relationships with ourselves and others and help us develop clarity and speak confidently. When we can release the blockages of this chakra, we become more expressive and more open-minded toward new ideas and perspectives. The openness of the Vishuddha Chakra can help us accept what comes our way throughout life's journey with a light heart and better outcomes.

The throat chakra.
https://pixabay.com/es/illustrations/azul-claro-vishuddha-chakra-mandala-1340078/

A. Symbol and Sanskrit Name

Vishuddha is the Sanskrit name for the throat chakra and is represented by a sixteen-petaled lotus flower. Its Sanskrit name translates to "purification," and it is located at the base of the throat.

B. Role and Benefits

The Vishuddha chakra governs our way of speaking, thinking, listening, and communicating with others. We can express ourselves with clarity and confidence when its energy is balanced. It also helps us to stay open-minded about new ideas and perspectives. Other benefits include improved relationships, better communication, and an overall increase in self-confidence.

C. Color, Sound, and Mantra

Vishuddha is associated with the color blue and the sound "Ham." Its mantra is "I Speak." Practicing this mantra will help to open up your throat chakra and release blockages.

D. Blockage Symptoms

When Vishuddha is blocked or out of balance, we may feel like our communication is stifled and restricted. We can also experience difficulty in speaking the truth and expressing our opinions, as well as having difficulty in listening to others. Physical symptoms of blockages can include throat pain, neck tension, and laryngitis.

E. Clear Chakra Sensations

When Vishuddha is balanced, we feel more open and receptive toward others' ideas and perspectives. We can easily express ourselves confidently and clearly. To open this chakra, practice yoga postures that focus on stretching the neck and throat area. However, the most crucial step is to work on releasing any unexpressed emotions or thoughts you may be holding onto. Acknowledge them and allow yourself to express your truth without fear.

Ajna: The Third Eye Chakra

Ajna is a vital energy point in many yogic practices, commonly called the *third eye chakra*. It is traditionally believed to open up one's psychic potential and sharpen intuition and inner knowledge. When balanced, this chakra can lead to a higher perception and understanding of ourselves, our relationships, and the world around us. To balance this particular energy point, it's essential to focus on cultivating clarity and trusting our wisdom. Through breath work, meditation, and self-reflection, we can begin to understand how we process and interpret information through Ajna's pathway for spiritual growth. Once opened, it allows for a true merger in deeper meditation states. The unspoken messages are heard clearly in the individual's consciousness.

The third eye chakra.
https://pixabay.com/es/illustrations/azul-chakra-mandala-meditaci%c3%b3n-1310076/

A. Symbol and Sanskrit Name

A two-petaled lotus flower represents *Ajna*. Its Sanskrit name translates to "command" or "perception," and it is located between the eyebrows.

B. Role and Benefits

The Ajna Chakra governs our intuition, imagination, wisdom, and perception of truth. When its energy is balanced, we can access a higher level of understanding and clarity. It helps us to connect with our inner knowledge and tap into our psychic potential. Benefits include improved intuition, better decision-making, creativity, and sharper concentration.

C. Color, Sound, and Mantra

Ajna is associated with the color indigo and the sound "Aum." Its mantra is "I See." Practicing this mantra will help to open up your third eye chakra and release blockages.

D. Blockage Symptoms

When Ajna is blocked or out of balance, we may have difficulty understanding our intuition and trusting our inner wisdom. We can also feel disconnected from our spiritual paths and find it hard to focus on the bigger picture. Physical symptoms of blockages can include tension headaches, fatigue, and difficulty in making decisions.

E. Clear Chakra Sensations

When Ajna is balanced, we have greater clarity and understanding of ourselves and others. We become more intuitive and can make decisions with confidence. To open this chakra, practice yoga postures focusing on the area between the eyebrows or a gentle head massage to help soothe any tension. Develop your inner wisdom and trust yourself by listening to your intuition; this will provide a solid foundation for understanding the deeper layers of Ajna.

Sahasrara: The Crown Chakra

The crown chakra is the highest energy point in the body and is located right at the top of the head. Known as *Sahasrara*, it represents enlightenment, spiritual connection, and our higher self. When opened, we can access a higher level of consciousness and experience a deeper connection to our spiritual nature.

The crown chakra.
https://pixabay.com/es/illustrations/violeta-blanco-chakra-1340083/

A. Symbol and Sanskrit Name

A thousand-petaled lotus flower represents *Sahasrara*; its Sanskrit name translates to "thousandfold" or "limitless." It is located at the top of the head and symbolizes enlightenment and spiritual connection.

B. Role and Benefits

The crown chakra is the highest energy point in the body and governs our spirituality, understanding of ourselves, and our connection with a higher power. When balanced, it helps us to connect deeply with our inner wisdom and access higher levels of consciousness. Benefits include improved intuition, greater clarity, enhanced creativity, and spiritual connection.

C. Color and Sound

Sahasrara is associated with purple or white and the sound "Aum." Its mantra is "I See." Repeating this mantra will help to open up your crown chakra and release any blockages you may be experiencing.

D. Blockage Symptoms

When the crown chakra is blocked or out of balance, we can experience feelings of disconnection from our spiritual paths and a lack of direction in life. We may feel disconnected from our higher power or have difficulty trusting our inner wisdom. Physical symptoms of blockages can include insomnia, headaches, and mental fatigue.

E. Clear Chakra Sensations

When the crown chakra is balanced, we feel connected to a higher power and have an overall clarity of our spiritual purpose. To open this chakra, practice yoga postures focusing on the top of the head or gently massage. Spend some time in nature and connect with your surroundings, opening up the crown chakra and providing a spiritual connection.

We can access our inner wisdom that can guide us through life by harnessing and understanding the chakras' power. Working on balancing each of the chakras will help to bring harmony into our lives and tap into our full potential. It is a lifelong journey of self-discovery and spiritual growth.

The practice of awakening and balancing the chakras through yoga, meditation, massage, and other holistic healing modalities can help to bring balance into our lives, reduce stress levels, and help us to reach our highest potential. Understanding the chakras' power allows us to access our inner wisdom that can guide us through life. With practice, we can awaken and balance the energy of each chakra to achieve a state of harmony and well-being.

By understanding the roles of the various chakras, we learn how to open them up and harness their power for greater spiritual growth. We must begin by understanding the power of the Kundalini energy and how it affects each chakra and its associated roles. By awakening this energy, we open ourselves to a new world of spiritual exploration and growth. Once we understand each chakra's role in our lives, we can begin to explore ways to awaken and balance the energy of each chakra to achieve a state of harmony and well-being!

Chapter 3: Preparing the Chakras for the Snake

The chakras are powerful energy centers, each governing different parts of our physical, mental, and emotional well-being. When out of balance or blocked, they can lead to a range of issues. Keeping your chakras balanced and healthy is essential to experiencing a sense of well-being and maintaining emotional, mental, and spiritual equilibrium. To ensure this balance, it is necessary to regularly cleanse and unblock your chakras. Regular cleansing removes negative energy and allows positive energy to flow freely. Unblocking the chakras ensures that the energy pathways remain open so that energy can continuously circulate through all seven centers in the body.

Preparing the chakras for cleansing and unblocking is a critical part of the process. This can be done through disciplines such as meditation, breathwork, mantras, visualization, yoga, or other physical activity. This chapter will guide you through how to cleanse and unblock each chakra. Following the methods outlined here, you can balance your chakras and align with your highest self.

Opening the Root Chakra

The root chakra is a powerful energy point found at the base of the spine and serves as a grounding force in all aspects of life. Opening the root chakra clears any energetic blocks that might be present and re-aligns our inner connection toward stability, security, and balance. It allows any emotions that may have been pushed away or suppressed to *rise*. Ultimately, this helps us to better connect with our bodies and have open conversations about what we need to feel secure and grounded. Working with this chakra can improve resilience, strength, and creativity, making it integral for those looking for an overall feeling of healthiness on their journey of self-discovery.

Diet Advice/Detox

Root chakra detoxing focuses on providing stability and a feeling of being grounded both emotionally and in life. Several simple diet tips can help you open this vital energy center in your body.

- Start by adding more root vegetables to your diet, like potatoes, carrots, onions, and sweet potatoes.
- Including warming spices such as cumin and cardamom is another dietary addition to help stimulate the root chakra's energetic flow.
- Eating freshly prepared meals that are nutrient-rich and starting with a healthy base of vegetables will help to provide the foundation for a balanced root chakra.

Lifestyle Changes

Making conscious changes to your lifestyle can positively affect your emotional and physical health, particularly when it comes to opening the root chakra. Some simple ways to promote root chakra health include:

- Spending more time outdoors
- Staying connected with people you trust
- Eating naturally nutritious foods
- Engaging in physical activities you enjoy
- Setting healthy boundaries
- Allowing yourself time for rest.

Taking care of ourselves creates a ripple effect that can help us face personal and professional challenges with greater resiliency. Nothing can be gained from overworking or getting stuck in unhealthy behaviors. Making these adjustments can be challenging initially, but committing to a healthier lifestyle is an invaluable opportunity for self-growth and development.

Asanas/Yoga Poses

Opening the root chakra through yoga postures can be powerful and effective. One of the best ways to begin is by standing flat on the floor and getting into the mountain pose. This simple asana grounds you and establishes your connection with the physical world, creating a foundation of awareness. From there, you can explore postures like squats and forward folds, keeping the knees soft and conscious, focusing on connecting with your breath. Seated postures that stretch and massage along the spine, such as those found in cat-cow, can also help open up your feeling of belonging in physical space.

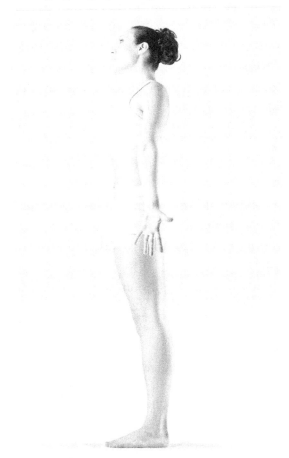

Mountain pose.
Mr. Yoga, CC BY-SA 4.0 <https://creativecommons.org/licenses/by-sa/4.0>, via Wikimedia Commons https://commons.wikimedia.org/wiki/File:Mr-yoga-mountain-pose-1.jpg

Cleansing the Sacral Chakra

Cleansing the sacral chakra is a powerful way to unlock creativity, passion, and sensuality in your life. It is essential for ushering in emotion-driven activities that can deepen relationships and calm anxieties about responsibility. Practicing self-reflection is a great way to start any journey toward cleansing this chakra. This can be done by journaling or meditating on who you are, the kind of life you want to lead, and how your values relate to it. Regular physical activities such as yoga or dance can open up blocked energies around this area in our bodies. Finally, listening to music, painting, and decorating with bright colors all help to enhance the connection we have with ourselves and others, allowing creative energy to flow more freely.

Diet Advice/Detox

In terms of dietary advice, sacral chakra detoxing requires plenty of hydration. Drinking enough water allows the body to flush out toxins and remain properly hydrated. Here are some other sacral chakra-friendly dietary tips:

- Increase your intake of oranges and other citrus fruits containing Vitamin C.
- Include foods that are high in antioxidants, such as blueberries and dark chocolate.
- Consume more omega-3 fatty acids found in salmon, flaxseed, and walnuts.
- Eating foods rich in magnesium and calcium, like leafy greens, bananas, nuts, and seeds, can help to further balance the sacral chakra.

Lifestyle Changes

Making conscious lifestyle changes, such as prioritizing self-care and allowing yourself to explore different creative outlets, can be a great way to get the sacral chakra moving. Taking time out from a hectic schedule to simply relax can be incredibly helpful in getting yourself to connect with your emotions on a deeper level. Here are some other great lifestyle tips for activating the sacral chakra:

- Take a bath or shower in Epsom salts to create an atmosphere of peace and relaxation.

- Engage in activities that bring joy and pleasure, such as walking outdoors or listening to music.
- Explore new creative projects and make time for hobbies that you truly enjoy.
- Create a supportive environment by surrounding yourself with positive and uplifting people.

Asanas/Yoga Poses

When it comes to finding the right poses for opening up the sacral chakra, focus on postures that stretch and massage along the lower back and hips. Forward folds are especially beneficial, as they can help to release tension in the body that has been blocked from lack of movement. The goddess pose is one of the best poses for this chakra, as it simultaneously opens up both the hips and the sacral area. Supported bridge and fire log poses are also excellent postures for stimulating the sacral chakra.

Goddess pose.
https://pixahive.com/photo/utka%E1%B9%ADa-ko%E1%B9%87asana-goddess-pose/

Unblocking the Solar Plexus Chakra

Our solar plexus chakra is the energy center in our bodies that greatly impacts how we feel. When blocked, we can be overwhelmed with fear, self-doubt, and anxiety, making it hard to face our inner truth. There are many ways to unblock this chakra, like meditation and yoga, but sometimes we need more of an abundance mindset shift by recognizing the good things in life and doing the things that make us happy. Pursuing positive thinking, maintaining healthy relationships, and actively practicing self-love assists us in reclaiming our power and opens us up to new opportunities – helping us shine from the inside out.

Diet Advice/Detox

When it comes to cleansing this chakra, the best advice is to flush out toxins. Start by drinking plenty of water to stay hydrated and flush out the gut. Eating plenty of fruits and vegetables while reducing your intake of processed foods can help to increase energy and improve digestion. Here are some other dietary tips to consider:

- Include more leafy greens in your meals, such as spinach and kale.
- Increase your intake of high-fiber foods like oats and brown rice.
- Snack on seeds, nuts, and legumes such as lentils or chickpeas.
- Eating lighter, more organic meals that contain healing spices like turmeric can also be beneficial.

Lifestyle Changes

Making lifestyle changes focusing on self-care and positive thinking can also help unblock the solar plexus chakra. Connecting with nature by taking a walk in the park or simply soaking up some sunshine can be incredibly relaxing and help balance this chakra. Here are some other lifestyle tips to consider:

- Look out for positive affirmations and mantras that resonate with you.
- Take up a hobby or activity that you find enjoyable, such as painting or baking.
- Forgive yourself and others for any mistakes made in the past.
- Practicing yoga, meditation, and deep breathing exercises can be incredibly beneficial.

Asanas/Yoga Poses

When finding the right poses for opening up the solar plexus chakra, focus on energizing and uplifting postures. Sun salutations are an excellent choice, as they help awaken the body and stir energy from within.

Standing poses stretching the spine and opening up the chest, such as warrior I and II, are also great for this chakra. Boat pose, bow pose, and upward facing dog can help to increase flexibility and give the midsection a gentle massage. Finally, the corpse pose is helpful for creating mindfulness and giving your body a chance to relax and recharge.

Sun salutation.
Mr. Yoga, CC BY-SA 4.0 <https://creativecommons.org/licenses/by-sa/4.0>, via Wikimedia Commons https://commons.wikimedia.org/wiki/File:Mr-yoga-sun_salutation_1.jpg

Rebalancing the Heart Chakra

Healing and rebalancing the heart chakra requires patience, awareness, and commitment. The fourth chakra is the bridge between our physical world and spiritual self. Connecting these two aspects of our being brings balance to daily life, which is necessary for overall health and well-being. To open the heart chakra, mindfulness is an essential element. Focus on love and compassion for oneself and others, express emotions freely, act out of kindness, and incorporate yoga postures that stimulate energy flow through the heart. Each of these processes connects with our inner truth to heal any blockages or traumas that prevent us from fully expressing ourselves.

Diet Advice/Detox

To open the heart chakra, focusing on detoxing and nourishing the body is beneficial. While it is crucial to maintain a healthy diet, certain foods can help with cleansing and opening the heart chakra. Here are a few tips to consider:

- Increase your intake of whole grains, such as quinoa and buckwheat.
- Include lots of leafy greens such as spinach, kale, and Swiss chard.
- Including more green vegetables in your diet, such as broccoli and spinach, can help to promote detoxification.
- Eat foods that are rich in antioxidants, like berries or dark chocolate.

Lifestyle Changes

Making lifestyle changes that focus on self-love and kindness can help to unblock the heart chakra. It is important to practice compassion and forgive oneself and others. Here are some helpful tips to consider:

- Engage in activities that make you feel connected with yourself, such as journaling and meditation.
- Surround yourself with people that make you feel valued and appreciated.
- Do something nice for someone else, even if it's something small.
- Take time for yourself and do things that make you feel happy and relaxed, such as listening to music or going for a walk.

Asanas/Yoga Poses

When it comes to finding the right poses for opening up the heart chakra, focus on cleansing and calming postures. Heart openers such as cobra, wheel, and bridge pose can stir up energy in the chest and awaken the heart. Backbends such as upward bow pose, camel, and bow pose can create a strong connection between the heart and back body. Finally, gentle inversions such as supported shoulder stands, legs up the wall, and fish poses are all beneficial for releasing tension from the chest and inviting harmony into the heart.

Cobra pose.

Purifying the Throat Chakra

The throat chakra, also known as the Vishuddha, is represented by the color blue and governs communication and self-expression. When this area of our being is unbalanced or "clogged," our ability to express ourselves honestly and confidently may be blocked. To purify your throat chakra, it is best to commit to a daily practice of vocalizing mantras, affirmations, or simply saying out loud things that you need to express but are afraid to. Doing this, even for a few minutes each day, can help identify areas in which communication needs healing in your life so that you may be able to work towards achieving a full balance within your throat chakra.

Diet Advice/Detox

The throat chakra is connected with the thyroid gland, which is responsible for regulating metabolism and energy levels. Eating foods that are beneficial to both the throat and the thyroid can be helpful in cleansing and opening the throat chakra. Here are a few tips to consider:

- Increase your intake of iodine-rich foods such as seaweed, eggs, and seafood.
- Include plenty of water-rich foods like cucumbers, celery, and melons.

• Eat foods that are high in antioxidants.

Lifestyle Changes

In addition to diet, lifestyle changes can also open and cleanse the throat chakra. Here are some helpful tips to consider:

- Take time for creative outlets, such as writing or music, to help you express yourself and your feelings.

- Make a conscious effort to be mindful of the words that come out of your mouth and practice speaking truthfully, without judgment.

- Get in touch with your spiritual side and meditate or practice yoga to help open up the throat chakra.

Asanas/Yoga Poses

When it comes to finding the right poses for opening up the throat chakra, focus on gentle and calming postures. Neck openers such as cat/cow, shoulder stand, and fish pose can help to release tension from the neck area, which is connected to the throat chakra. Backbends such as bow, camel, and cobra pose can create space in the chest area and awaken the throat chakra. Inversions such as a supported shoulder stand and legs up the wall can also balance the throat chakra by providing a sense of comfort and peace. Finally, supine twisting poses such as half lord of the fishes and revolved triangle can purify and open the throat chakra.

Fish pose.
Mr. Yoga, CC BY-SA 4.0 <https://creativecommons.org/licenses/by-sa/4.0/deed.en> via Wikimedia Commons https://commons.wikimedia.org/wiki/File:Mr-yoga-fish-pose.jpg

Illuminating the Third Eye Chakra

Many people turn to the illumination of their third eye chakra as an essential step in strengthening themselves spiritually. By tapping into the energies associated with this area, one can find greater insight, balance, and clarity in their life. It is believed that accessing this energy center boosts intuition and opens us up to experiencing our true potential. With regular meditation, deep relaxation (or even visualizing a bright white light in the center of our forehead), we can slowly but surely start to become aware of what lies behind our physical body on a spiritual level. Ultimately, these techniques are powerful tools for connecting to our inner wisdom, which takes us on a journey of self-discovery and transformation.

Diet Advice/Detox

As the third eye chakra is associated with sight, eating foods that are good for our eyesight can cleanse and open this area of our being. To open the third eye chakra, try to eat foods high in Vitamin A, such as carrots and spinach. In addition, try to limit your intake of processed or sugary food as these can damage our eyesight. Here are some helpful tips to consider:

- Increase your intake of Vitamin A-rich foods such as carrots, spinach, and sweet potatoes.
- Avoid processed or sugary foods.
- Eat plenty of dark leafy greens such as kale, arugula, and collards.

Lifestyle Changes

Certain lifestyle changes can help open up the third eye chakra as well. To get the most benefit out of this practice, try to focus on activities that involve being mindful and present such as meditation and yoga. Here are some helpful tips to consider:

- Take time for yourself each day to meditate or practice yoga.
- Make a conscious effort to be mindful and present in all of your activities throughout the day.
- Get into nature whenever possible, as this can help to ground you and awaken your third eye chakra.

Asanas/Yoga Poses

When finding the right poses for opening up the third eye chakra, focus on calming and uplifting postures. Forward folds such as seated forward bend and child's pose can release any tension from the head area connected to the third eye chakra. Inversions such as a supported shoulder stand and legs up the wall can balance this area by providing a sense of comfort and peace. Finally, supine poses, such as in transcendental meditation and *nadi shodhan pranayama,* can purify and open the third eye chakra.

Child's pose.
https://pixabay.com/es/photos/yoga-childs-pose-asana-2959214/

Awakening the Crown Chakra

Activating the crown chakra can be the catalyst for a life-altering experience of personal growth and transformation. Through this sacred process of introspection, our inner light can become brighter and more balanced. To awaken the crown, we must take a journey inwards. This includes examining our beliefs, becoming mindful of how we interact with others, and setting aside time for spiritual practice or meditation. As we do this work and let go of what no longer serves us, our awareness and understanding expand, which allows opportunities for personal growth. Our connection to divine energy is strengthened as we begin to open up the pathways within ourselves, allowing love, peace, and bliss to infuse every part of our being.

Diet Advice/Detox

Cleansing the crown chakra requires a mindful approach to diet. To spark vitality in this area, one should focus on eating light, fresh, organic foods rich in vitamins and minerals. Foods that contain phytonutrients (compounds produced by plants that provide health benefits to the body), such as berries, leafy greens, and cruciferous vegetables, are especially good for this area. Here are some helpful tips to consider:

- Eat a diet rich in dark leafy greens, berries, and cruciferous vegetables.
- Choose organic fruits and vegetables when possible.
- Limit your intake of processed foods and sugar.

Lifestyle Changes

In addition to diet, lifestyle plays an important role in activating the crown chakra. Regular exercise and relaxation are necessary to optimize the flow of energy between the chakras. Adding a simple stretching routine or yoga practice to your daily life can open up the pathways of energy and bring balance. Here are some helpful tips to consider:

- Take some time each day to practice simple stretching or yoga poses.
- Engage in activities that bring you joy, such as journaling or walking in nature.
- Make an effort to meditate or practice mindful breathing every day.

Asanas/Yoga Poses

Certain yoga postures specifically target the crown chakra. These postures help open up the energy pathways, allowing for the free energy flow between the mind and body. Headstand (Sirsasana) stimulates the crown chakra and encourages balance and clarity. Other postures that help awaken this area are the lotus pose (Padmasana), and corpse pose (Savasana). These poses help relax and open up the higher chakras providing a sense of oneness and peace.

Sirsasana pose.
https://www.pexels.com/photo/strong-woman-doing-sirsasana-posture-6454199/

As you work through this cleansing journey, remember to be gentle with yourself and stay open-minded. With consistency, patience, and perseverance, you can tap into the power of your energy and awaken the vibrant life force within you. By taking a mindful approach to diet, lifestyle, and yoga practices, we can awaken the crown chakra and experience a deeper level of spiritual connection. Through regular practice, we can begin to expand our consciousness and experience a more harmonious balance in our lives!

Chapter 4: Pranayama and Drishti: Focus and Breathe

Kundalini meditation and yoga are powerful tools that bridge our physical bodies to the energetic realm. Through intentional breathwork and posture, stagnant energy stored in the body is released while new, vibrant energy is called in. Practicing Kundalini meditation and yoga allows us to confront whatever riddles lie within ourselves and come out on a transformative journey of self-discovery. It opens up the opportunity to rediscover who we are at each level of consciousness, ultimately leading us back to our inner truth of oneness.

The ability to focus and breathe is fundamental to effective meditation.
https://unsplash.com/photos/rOn57CBgyMo

Kundalini yoga combines simple yet deeply embedded ancient practices with mantras used to anchor your divine creativity and power. This chapter focuses on two key components of Kundalini meditation and yoga, including Drishti (the eye gaze) and Pranayama (the regulation of the breath through certain techniques and exercises). It provides an understanding of both the eye gaze and the proper breathing techniques that can be used to support the journey of Kundalini meditation and yoga. By mastering the basics of these two components, you'll be able to take your Kundalini practice deeper and create the space for profound transformation.

Drishti - The Eye Gaze

Drishti is an integral concept in the practice of yoga. The directed gaze of awareness and purpose maintains focus on a particular point throughout a yoga practice. Practicing with Drishti helps us stay mindful and connected with our breath, our physical movements, and *ourselves*. By providing stability to the spine and calming the brain, this powerful tool takes us beyond the self-doubt and distractions that could obstruct us from deepening our connection with each pose. The concept of Drishti also teaches us to be conscious of what we gaze on in our lives outside yoga practice; as has been said, "we become what we behold." Drishti can help direct our inner eye in discovering what matters most to us in life.

A. What Is Drishti?

To be successful in Kundalini meditation and yoga, it is essential to understand what *Drishti* is. The word originates in Sanskrit and can be translated as "the eye gaze." It is the intentional and mindful direction of our sight. By using Drishti in yoga practice, we can keep our mind focused on a particular point, allowing us to connect with the breath and move through postures with intention. Iyengar Yoga, a type of modern yoga, defines the Drishti as "a gaze to bring awareness to its direction." While practicing Drishti, the eyes can be open or closed depending on the individual's preference.

B. Uses of Drishti in Kundalini Meditation and Yoga

Drishti stabilizes the mind and helps us attain mental clarity by allowing us to hold our concentration on one object for some time. We can further connect with our spiritual selves by focusing on one object during meditation. Using Drishti encourages conscious breathing to remain in each posture longer, increasing its benefits. Some kriyas (a specific set of exercises) require practitioners to gaze upward, downward, or outward towards horizons to align the body's energies and draw them inward toward the third eye center. Together, these practices create an environment that allows for more profound stillness and introspection.

1. Finding Focus

By focusing on energy and awareness, practitioners enter a meditative state and can begin to experience the full power of their practice. By concentrating on silent mantras or other stimuli, we can fully employ our physical and spiritual forces to reap all the benefits of Kundalini meditation and yoga. Although sometimes difficult for some newcomers to find such focus, when you have achieved it, it can lead to a deep understanding and appreciation of mediation practices.

2. Creating a Balanced Energy Flow

By gently focusing on different points in meditation or yoga postures, we can direct the energy that otherwise would be easily scattered throughout the body. This leads to greater internal awareness, as well as better mental clarity and emotional stability. Using Drishti during Kundalini meditation can create a deep meditative state, giving us access to the always-available inner resources of intuition and creativity. In summary, Drishti helps create a balanced energy flow that brings newfound vitality and healing into our lives.

3. Aligning Your Attention with Your Intentions

Using the visual power of Drishti to align your attention with your intentions is crucial in Kundalini meditation and yoga. When you focus on this practice, it gives you clarity and direction in life. With this type of focus and visualization, you gain deeper insight into yourself and more control over how you react to different experiences. As a result, your life can become more harmonious and balanced as your body posture changes and your energy aligns with your goals. These meditation techniques may be difficult at first, but once they become a regular part of your day, their influences will be transformative!

C. Specific Eye Focuses

Kundalini meditation and yoga are both ancient practices that involve specific eye focuses on unlocking a rich spiritual potential. In Kundalini meditation, practitioners concentrate their gaze on a single point while in a meditative practice designed to increase energy flow and inner awareness. Through this method, practitioners may experience a transcendent state of mental clarity, heightened intuition, and improved overall health and well-being.

Similarly, in yoga poses such as Padmasana or Mandukasana, practitioners are instructed to focus their eyes on an external object, typically one that connects them to the physical world. This practice, *trataka* (ir eye gazing), grounds the practitioner and fosters a deeper connection with nature. This simple yet profound practice allows yogis to deepen their concentration and obtain something greater than physical strength, a connection with divine understanding and peace within oneself. Through these specific eye focuses within Kundalini meditation and yoga, practitioners can access vast inner resources they never knew they had.

1. Brow Point

Developing your focus at the point between your brows leads to increased clarity of insight and intuition, which can then be used to manifest change and transformation in life. Learn how to practice the fine art of honing this mental acuity through pranayama or breath exercises, such as kriyas, chanting, and visualization. You'll find that when you train yourself to become aware of the brow point during your Kundalini meditations and yoga classes, you'll access a deeper level of stillness within, connecting you with a reservoir of inner strength and power.

2. Tip of the Nose

As Kundalini practitioners learn more about meditating, they access even deeper levels of consciousness by focusing their attention on the tip of the nose. Not only does this action increase sensory acuity and spatial awareness, but deriving from ancient yogic teachings, this technique improves how people respond to external stimuli and manage stress better. Regardless of your experience level or background in Yoga, learning how to focus your energy on the tip of your nose can bring great mental clarity, an essential piece for any successful Kundalini practice.

3. Chin

The practice of yoga and Kundalini meditation involves the specific use of eye focus for profound spiritual awakening. Focusing on the chin specifically, known as Chin Dharana, is a way to bring awareness to the third eye area that rests in the middle of the forehead, allowing connection with a higher level of consciousness. Though different techniques are required to activate this energy, a common practice among yogis is gazing between the eyebrows, corresponding with a rhythmical focus at the chin. This technique prepares one's body and mind for entering deep meditative states and encourages intensely powerful realizations that are an essential part of Kundalini yoga, making Chin Dharana an extremely powerful and valuable meditation technique.

4. Crown Chakra

The crown chakra, or Sahasrara, is the seventh major chakra in the body and governs wisdom, understanding, enlightenment, and connection to our inner divine self. Focusing your gaze on this chakra can help close the gap between the physical and spiritual realms. Focusing your eyes on a candle flame, an image of divinity, or even your thumb can ground you while providing an avenue to explore these higher realms. Whether you practice Kundalini meditation or yoga regularly or just when relaxing, these eye focuses can be beneficial tools for ultimate relaxation and awareness of your divine energy.

5. 1/10th Open

To tap into the Kundalini energy, practitioners of Kundalini meditation and Yoga use an eye-focus technique known as "1/10th Open," in which they keep their eyelids slightly open while mantras, visual images, or awareness to sensations of breath or an aspect of the physical body is present. This is a way to create a balance between being grounded in reality and creating mental space for concentrating the mind and connecting energetically to expand vision and creativity. 1/10th Open focuses on focusing attention while grounding the senses in physical reality through regular breathing techniques, eventually leading practitioners to newfound clarity, insight, and understanding.

Pranayama (The Proper Breathing)

Pranayama, or proper breathing, is integral to many types of yoga practice. This technique is used to regulate and control breath, improving both physical and mental health. Through this practice, one can increase their lung capacity, raise energy levels and create a sense of calmness. Proper breathing also improves our connection with the Universe and its inexhaustible energy source. With regular practice and dedication, a yogi can reach higher states of concentration through Pranayama and ultimately deepen their connection with the cosmos. Even beginners can start to see some benefits in just a few weeks if they stay consistent in their efforts.

A. What Is Pranayama?

Originating in India and formed from two Sanskrit words, Pranayama is an ancient practice associated with yoga. The two words combined to form Pranayama are *"Prana,"* meaning life force or breath, and *"Ayama,"* meaning control. Pranayama is a yogic technique that involves controlling and regulating the breath to improve one's physical health, mental clarity, and overall well-being. It involves breathing exercises to create a balance between the physical body and the mind.

B. Pranayama's Importance in Kundalini Awakening

Pranayama is a powerful tool for spiritual advancement and Kundalini awakening. By controlling the breath, one can create new energy pathways that unlock dormant energies within the body, allowing them to rise to bring greater consciousness and spiritual growth. Pranayama is also an effective way to reduce physical and mental tension so that meditation flows more easily. When combined with visualization practices, Ppranayama can open up new avenues of awakening the Kundalini force that lies dormant within everyone. This way, we can build stronger connections between our bodies, minds, and souls to get greater clarity and insight into truth and reality.

1. Connecting to Your Core

In Kundalini Awakening, Pranayama breathwork plays an essential role. Connecting you to your core and establishing a strong link between your spiritual and physical self, Pranayama is the first step in awakening the dormant energy within. Through conscious breathing exercises and cleansing of your mind and body, you begin to experience greater clarity, deeper concentration, and a stronger purpose. Pranayama allows you to tap into new depths of self-awareness and transformation that ultimately profoundly impact your life's journey. As you take control of your respiration, a higher level of consciousness and a renewed connection with yourself and the divine energy around you can be attained.

2. Increasing Awareness and Focus

The ancient practice of Pranayama is a cornerstone connection between mind and body. It increases one's awareness and focus. This practice can positively affect physical health and awaken the dormant energies in the chakras known as Kundalini. Pranayama enlightens the breath while deepening awareness of one's inner self. Through Pranayama, practitioners can learn how to be aware of their thoughts and feelings, which leads to healing and potential spiritual awakening. Regular practice brings clarity to the body-mind connection, encouraging further exploration of meditation techniques and enabling people to channel their human potential for personal transformation and growth.

3. Energizing Your Meditation

Pranayama works at a cellular level to release toxins and can be used to tap into unlimited reserves of energy that permeate our meditation practice and aid in the awakening process. During a Pranayama session, we can eliminate blockages in our energetic body, allowing vital energy forces like chi and kundalini to flow freely and stir up spiritual progress by activating such things as chakras and karmic seed impressions. Meditators can reduce stress levels by developing greater control over their breath and mastering pranayama techniques while expanding their receptive abilities, leading to deeper states of meditation with higher spiritual payoffs.

C. Kundalini Breathing Exercises

Kundalini breathing exercises are a powerful tool for achieving peace and clarity within. These exercises have been used in spiritual practice for centuries to balance inner energies and cultivate good health, mental strength, and emotional resilience. They involve regulated breathing techniques that combine breath control with movement, postures, and meditation. By focusing on the breath, you can become aware of your inner emotions, leading to increased self-awareness and self-trust. Through systematic kundalini breathing exercises, practitioners feel more connected to their spiritual cores and more capable of cultivating positive states of mind.

1. Alternate Nostril Breathing

Alternate Nostril Breathing, also known as Nadi Shodhana Pranayama, is a potent Kundalini breathing exercise that works to balance the energies of the body and calm the mind by completing single full breaths through alternating nostrils. By controlling your inhalation and exhalation speed, you can bring your body into a state of greater balance. During this exercise, your breath creates a sound as it proceeds from one side and then back again, promoting relaxation. The process oxygenates all body parts, bringing clarity to our minds and increasing focus and concentration while reducing stress levels.

Steps:

1. Begin by sitting comfortably with your spine erect and eyes closed.
2. Place your left hand on your knee in a comfortable and relaxed position.
3. Place your right thumb over your right nostril and your ring finger over the left nostril.

4. Inhale deeply and slowly through your right nostril, then close it with your thumb.

5. Release your ring finger, and exhale slowly through your left nostril.

6. Remain in this position for a few moments, keeping your eyes closed.

7. Inhale deeply and slowly through your left nostril, then close it with your ring finger.

8. Release your thumb, and exhale slowly through your right nostril.

9. Remain in this position for a few moments, keeping your eyes closed.

10. Repeat this cycle for up to ten minutes and then stop, taking a few moments to relax in the stillness of your practice.

2. Breath of Fire

Breath of Fire is one of the most powerful breathing techniques to reduce physical and mental stress. It circulates your energy, cleanses your organs, and encourages increased prana (life force). This practice requires a smooth rhythmical pattern of conscious breathwork that alternates between equal lengths of inhalation and exhalation. Regularly doing these exercises can make you more relaxed, patient, and focused. Not only does this breathing technique provide physical wellness benefits such as reduced anxiety, but it also clears mental blockages that can keep us stuck in patterns of behavior and thought that limit us.

Steps:

1. Start in a comfortable seated position.

2. Place one hand on your lower abdomen and the other on your chest.

3. Begin rapid, shallow breathing through the nose with equal-length inhalations and exhalations.

4. Focus on your breath, allowing it to flow continuously while keeping a steady rhythm.

5. Feel the breath rise and fall in your abdomen and chest, respectively.

6. Continue for up to two minutes and then stop, taking a few moments to relax in the stillness of your practice.

3. Ujjayi Pranayama

Ujjayi pranayama is an ancient practice of mindful breathing originating in the tradition of Kundalini yoga. It promotes mental clarity, calmness, and inner balance. The basic technique involves inhaling slowly and deeply through the nose while slightly constricting the throat muscles, creating a soft "ocean wave" sound known as Ujjayi breath. This type of breathing fosters relaxation and quiets the mind and body by bringing awareness to the present moment. Practicing Ujjayi pranayama reduces stress, opens the body's energy centers, and activates higher states of consciousness. It provides numerous physical, emotional, and spiritual benefits for both beginners and experienced practitioners.

Steps:

1. Begin by sitting comfortably with your spine erect and eyes closed.
2. Take a few moments to relax, focusing on the natural breath.
3. Begin to inhale and exhale through the nose, taking deep breaths that expand the lungs as you inhale and contract them as you exhale.
4. Focus on the sound of your breath as it passes through the throat and notice how this creates a soft "ocean wave" type of sound.
5. Continue for up to 5-10 minutes, then release and relax in the stillness of your practice.

4. Long, Deep Breathing

Long, deep breathing exercises can be amazingly physically, mentally, and spiritually beneficial. Kundalini breathing is among the most popular of these exercises, combining aspects of traditional Eastern yogic practices with a more modern Westernized focus on energy centers and chakras. On a physiological level, Kundalini breathing relaxes muscles and organs in the body while stimulating neural cortex activity and clearing any potential blockages. On an emotional level, it promotes feelings of peace, confidence, and joy. Likewise, many practitioners find that regular practice offers deeper spiritual insights and access to higher levels of consciousness.

Steps:

1. Begin in a comfortable seated position. Close your eyes and take a few moments to relax, focusing on the natural breath.
2. Inhale deeply and slowly through the nose, directing the breath to fill your lungs from bottom to top.

3. When you reach the fullest inhalation possible, pause and hold your breath for a few seconds.

4. Exhale slowly and deeply through the nose, releasing as much air as possible.

5. Repeat the cycle for up to 10 minutes, then release and relax in the stillness of your practice.

Drishti and pranayama can be used together or separately as part of your kundalini practice. These powerful techniques enhance relaxation, clear mental blockages, and promote higher states of consciousness. When practiced regularly, they can offer tremendous physical, emotional, and spiritual benefits that are well worth the effort. This chapter has provided a brief overview of these two techniques and the steps involved in practicing them. We hope this introduction helps inspire your exploration of Kundalini meditations and Pranayama breathing exercises. Happy awakening!

Chapter 5: Unlocking Energy with Mudras and Mantras

Mudras and mantras are two spiritual practices that yogis have used for centuries. Mudras involve forming special hand gestures to help cultivate inner peace and stimulate the Kundalini energy. Mantras are sacred words, phrases, or syllables that can be chanted or repeated silently in meditation to manifest positive change or amplify energy flow. When combined, mudras and mantras can open up the energy pathways throughout the body, allowing for deeper healing and transformation. They are powerful tools for releasing trapped emotions and restoring vibrant health, balance, and well-being.

Mudras and mantras help center your balance and focus.
https://unsplash.com/photos/n8L1VYaypcw

This chapter will cover the role of mudras and mantras in Kundalini awakening and yoga. It will also discuss their general benefits as well as provide a list of the most useful and potent mudras and mantras for practicing Kundalini yoga. The specific meanings and chakra activations of the Kundalini mantras will also be discussed. While mudras and mantras are deeply intertwined, this chapter will discuss them separately to better understand the practices. By the end of this chapter, you'll have a much deeper understanding of mudras and mantras and how to use them to awaken your Kundalini energy.

Mudras

Mudras are a type of hand gesture commonly seen in ancient Indian art, such as statues and paintings. Mudras tap into the power of prana, or life energy, and have specific meanings that are thought to bring about physical health and spiritual insight. For example, the Abhaya Mudra conveys protection, courage, and blessings from the divine, Gyan Mudra aids in balance and enlightenment, Dharmachakra Mudra is an invocation for truth, and the Varada Mudra symbolizes charity. Surya Mudra is believed to improve metabolism, Añjali Mudra awakens compassion and humility, and Dhyana Mudra encourages meditation and connection. Practicing these mudras can be a powerful healing tool on all levels.

A. The Role and Concept of Mudras

Mudras represent several sacred meanings ranging from simple to complex and vary across cultures and practices. Like Hinduism's Namaskara mudra of greeting and respect for the teachings of yoga, these ritualistic symbols are infused with an inner power that helps invoke strong emotions associated with different spiritual concepts. Mudras offer a powerful path for achieving a personal connection to higher consciousness and understanding if used accurately and respectfully. Practitioners often use these meaningful postures in meditation or prayer to access greater insight or reflect on specific feelings toward inner truth or enlightenment.

B. Benefits of Mudras

Kundalini Yoga offers an array of benefits, from increased physical strength and stability to enhanced spiritual and emotional well-being. One of its unique aspects is the mudras that draw upon the body's energy, enabling practitioners to gain even more from their practice. These hand gestures can be used for various purposes, such as helping to control breath, balancing the chakras, and calming the mind. Used correctly, mudras can help Kundalini yoga practitioners reach a deep connection with themselves that is difficult to achieve through other forms of yoga or meditation. A consistent practice of using mudras in Kundalini yoga sessions creates a strong link between the mind and body while allowing a deeper understanding and acceptance of one's self.

1. Physical Benefits

One of the first steps a yogi will learn in Kundalini yoga is a set of mudras or hand positions. Each mudra has a particular meaning associated with it. But beyond the symbolism, one area in which Kundalini has excelled is unlocking specific bodily benefits through harnessing energy and movement, largely due to these helpful mudras. Just as our hands can be quite expressive when we're communicating verbally, they can also demonstrate healing power via these subtle shifts while practicing Kundalini yoga. By unlocking each chakra system, with different mudras representing each region within us, we understand which areas require more attention than others. This imaginative exploration increases circulation to promote healthier muscles and joints throughout the body while developing physical and emotional strength grounded in self-exploration!

2. Mental Benefits

One of the main ways to achieve self-awareness and create balance is by using mudras. Mudras reduce stress and anxiety, increase focus, boost creativity, and improve clarity in thinking. By bringing attention to the hands and nurturing mindfulness, mudras can bring us into a more grounded and present state of being. Furthermore, combining them with breath work can induce a meditative state that further opens us up to our inner wisdom. So, it's easy to see that, practiced regularly, mudras can significantly benefit our mental health.

3. Spiritual Benefits

One integral part of using mudras in Kundalini yoga is to increase spiritual energy throughout the body. Mudras redirect subtle energy within the body, clearing blockages and creating balance and harmony. Each mudra has spiritual benefits, allowing us to open our hearts and minds, helping us to enter a deep meditative state, commune with spirituality, and potentially bring about a heightened awareness as we move closer to enlightenment. Those who regularly practice Kundalini yoga and its accompanying mudras can experience profound spiritual growth as they deepen their physical and mental well-being.

C. Useful and Potent Mudras for Kundalini Yoga

Yoni Mudra, Bhairavi Mudra, and Shunya Mudra are three useful and potent mudras for activating Kundalini energies. Yoni Mudra symbolizes starting from the seed of creation and is meant to connect us with our spiritual essence. Bhairavi Mudra stimulates intuition, courage, enthusiasm, and creativity. It strengthens inner wisdom. On the other hand, Shunya Mudra focuses on stillness and clarity within ourselves. Several mudras can help us become more mindful of our breath, relaxation, centering, and concentration, all components of Kundalini yoga.

1. Kundalini Mudra

The powerful Kundalini Mudra opens the chakras in the body, allowing them to be filled with energy, and recognizes imbalances that need correcting. The fingers cover different points throughout the body, encouraging a tranquil yet alert flow of energy as if simultaneously charging all parts of your body. When using these mudras, you may notice a heightened sense of balance, clarity, and harmony that strengthens with each repetition or skillful movement. With consistent practice, the full benefits of Kundalini Mudras can truly be experienced!

2. Uddiyan Bandha

Uddiyan Bandha is a powerful mudra and yoga technique rooted in traditional Kundalini yoga. Uddiyan Bandha translates to flying or upward lock, which refers to the visceral lifts of the muscles in the stomach area that this mudra requires. It flushes stale energies and awakens creativity and positive energy. Practicing Uddiyan Bandha challenges you to reawaken your life force. It eliminates fatigue, anxiety, depression, and other negative emotions while promoting physical strength, agility, and resilience. It is an effective form of relaxation, encouraging deep breathing, which can help clear the mind and body of built-up stress. People who practice Uddiyan Bandha regularly have also reported benefits such as improved digestion and toned abdominal muscles. It can be integrated into any practice involving yoga flow or postures with ample rest time between exercises for greater mental and physical benefits.

3. Mahamudra

Mahamudra, developed by Yogi Bhajan and practiced worldwide, helps practitioners relax and become grounded during meditation. It is a useful way to access your body and soul's energy, allowing you to open up pathways that are closed off from everyday life. When practicing

Mahamudra regularly, one can find clarity and an overall sense of well-being within. Anyone who practices this mudra will experience profound shifts in their mental, physical, and spiritual health. The benefits of this mudra include a deeper connection with one's true potential, inner peace, and enhanced intuition. With consistent effort, you can reach powerful energetic states essential for healing on all levels. Given such magical properties, it is clear why Mahamudra has become so popular amongst those practicing Kundalini yoga today.

4. Apana Mudra

The Apana Mudra is another extremely beneficial and potent mudra pose for practicing Kundalini yoga. It is beneficial because it releases any stagnant energy in the body and promotes energy circulation from the lower abdomen toward the feet. With this pose, practitioners will get an increased awareness and grounding in their bodies and a greater connection between body and mind. Practicing this mudra regularly will enhance strength and flexibility, energize organs, purify the blood, improve digestion, balance hormones, and increase fertility. This balanced practice provides a feeling of empowering stability while stimulating creativity and boosting joy.

5. Gyana Mudra

The Gyana Mudra, also known as the Gyan Mudra or Jnana Mudra, is a crucial part of Kundalini yoga. It involves stretching your fingers so that your thumb and first two fingers form a circle, with the remaining fingers curling towards the palm. Also known as the "seal of knowledge," this potent mudra is believed to awaken inner wisdom and unlock intellectual power. Practitioners of Kundalini yoga use this mudra to enter a deep meditative state, resulting in increased concentration, clarity of thought, and higher states of consciousness. In addition to its spiritual benefits, Gyana Mudra reduces stress and induces relaxation, as well as relieves carpal tunnel-like issues caused by repetitive motions experienced by people doing typing or repetitive heavy work. In summary, Gyana Mudra is certainly a useful practice for those interested in advancing their physical well-being and spiritual awareness.

Mantras

Mantras are an ancient form of chanting used to connect with a higher power since the beginning of time. Each mantra has its individual significance and meaning, which can focus you on universal energy and help you reach a blissful meditation state. Mantras have no limits in terms of purpose and use, as they can be chanted to enter into the space of inner peace, channel the universe's energy, strengthen faith and willpower, or learn more about oneself. Regardless of the goal you try to achieve through your mantra practice, you're guaranteed to move towards a meaningful life filled with tranquility and harmony.

A. Prayers for Kundalini

Prayers for Kundalini are becoming increasingly popular for spiritual healing and growth. When used with prayer, the Kundalini energy is enhanced and can produce increased mental acuity, improved physical health, deeper spiritual connection, and more profound emotional clarity. Regular practice can open up doorways to new forms of self-awareness and a greater understanding of life's mysteries. Kundalini prayers have been used for centuries as a powerful tool in one's spiritual journey and can bring about both personal inner peace and worldly balance.

1. Kirtan Sohila

Kirtan Sohila is an ancient Sikh prayer for Kundalini energy and awakening of the soul. It is recited daily by Sikhs before going to bed. Kirtan Sohila gently washes away any worries and anxieties, bringing in a state of deep relaxation, peace, and calmness. Its divine words travel through the layers of the physical body and connect us directly to our true divine self, pure consciousness beyond time, space, and formlessness. One experiences a sense of union with the Universal Consciousness in its meditative chant. This blessing experience can bring well-being to one's life on all levels, physically, emotionally, mentally, spiritually, and transcendentally.

2. Guru Ram Das Prayer

Guru Ram Das is revered as the fourth Sikh Guru and chief of five beloved Gurus. His legacy connects us to an ancient devotional tradition of transformational Kundalini meditation. Through his inspiring words, he speaks to us still, particularly through the timeless prayer for Kundalini. This powerful mantra calls upon divine intervention to unlock the flow of spiritual energy within, expressing a desire to know freedom and find love in our hearts and souls. The results are profound, awakening the dormant spirit within, calming depression and fear, and enabling each individual to experience true fulfillment in life.

3. Vishnu Sahasranam

Vishnu Sahasranam, a prayer dedicated to Lord Vishnu, is believed to be powerful enough to awaken your dormant Kundalini energy. The prayer can help you tap into your inner strength and connects you with the divine force within you. By chanting it regularly, one can attain inner peace and clarity, as well as strengthen your connection with the divine source. Vishnu Sahasranam comprises 1000 different names of Lord Vishnu, each of which acts as a spiritual growth tool. Experienced Yogis suggest that this kind of practice gives positive results if practiced with sincerity, dedication, and attention. Doing so allows you to manifest your desires and appreciate life from a larger perspective.

B. Kundalini Mantras

Kundalini mantras are powerful chants believed to give practitioners an added spiritual boost when practiced regularly. These mantras also aim to open up the energy at the base of the spine, where the dormant Serpent Power lies. Although they are used as part of a particular style of yoga, their effect can be called on by anyone who has committed them to memory and meditated on their meaning. Some people also find that chanting these mantras in certain combinations and with certain sounds can benefit their physical, mental, and spiritual well-being. With many Kundalini mantras available, each practitioner can find one or several that resonate deeply with them and use them as part of their path to self-discovery.

1. Adi Mantra

Om Namo Guru Dev Namo

Meaning: "I bow to the Divine within myself, my guru."

Adi Mantra is used in meditation and yoga to activate divine energies, bringing us closer to the Divine. Through daily repetition of the Adi Mantra, its spiritual power works to balance our inner chakras, helping us tap into the infinite consciousness and spiritual strength that already exists within ourselves. Each cycle of this mantra brings energetic healing, allowing you to feel more connected and open to spiritual evolution. "Adi" translates to primordial nature in many cultures worldwide, reflecting the powerhouse of the healing potential that can be unlocked by activating the chakras through the Adi Mantra. As we journey on this path towards enlightenment and soul expansion, the regular practice of chanting the Adi Mantra allows us to relax more completely and deepen our spiritual understanding of ourselves and our relationships with others.

2. Mangala Charn Mantra

Aad Guray Nameh, Jugad Guray Nameh, Sat Guray Nameh, Siri Guru Devay Nameh

Meaning: "I bow to the primal guru, I bow to the wisdom throughout the ages, I bow to the true guru, I bow to great divine wisdom."

Mangala Charn Mantra is an ancient and powerful Kundalini mantra from the Upanishads that invoke Lord Shiva and Goddess Parvati to bring forth divine energy. The word "Mangala" means "auspicious," and it can invigorate the seven chakras for spiritual growth. This mantra brings greater peace, joy, clarity of purpose, and satisfaction by opening the heart to love and compassion. It can also assist in healing physical, emotional, psychological, and spiritual issues. Additionally, this mantra activates each chakra, connecting each area of one's life to that particular chakra, such as creativity or relationships, to move closer toward well-being. Therefore, chanting Mangala Charn Mantra is a powerful practice for true transformation.

3. Mul Mantra

Ek Onkar Sat Nam Karta Purakh Nirbhau Nirvair Akal Murat Ajuni Saibhang Gur Prasad

Meaning: "There is one Creator of all, truth is its name, doer of everything, fearless and without enmity, beyond time, beyond form and self-illuminated. May this be granted to us by Guru's Grace."

The *Mul Mantra*, or "root mantra," is an ancient Hindu one that has provided immense power and spiritual healing to seekers worldwide for centuries. Its poetic composition opens the gateway to a profound spiritual understanding while awakening our Kundalini Shakti. Translated from ancient Sanskrit, one of the meanings behind the Mul Mantra is "I open myself up to experience the Divine within." Its resonance activates the root chakra, is essential for good health and well-being, and releases any blockages along our spine to allow us to move through life with creativity and full presence. Participating in this ancient practice of gaining access to inner divinity and unlocking one's infinite potential is a special experience that can be cherished forever.

4. Shri Gayatri Mantra

Om Bhur Bhuva Swaha, Tat Savitur Varenyam, Bhargo Devasaya Dheemahi, Dhiyo Yo Nah Prachodayat

Meaning: "We meditate on the divine light of Savitur; may it inspire and illumine our minds and hearts."

Shri Gayatri Mantra is an ancient chant said to activate the third eye or Ajna Chakra. It has become a cornerstone in Kundalini yoga and meditation as it invokes universal wisdom and guides spiritual awakening within a practitioner. The mantra's deepening effects come from its many layers of meaning and resonance. Humbling, inspiring, and deeply powerful, this invocation brings many profound benefits, including mental clarity, improved sleep, increased intuition, enhanced concentration, and greater insight into the true nature of conscious awareness. With regular practice and other meditative lifestyle measures like diet and breathing exercises, practitioners can expect to experience profound transformation through their work with Shri Gayatri Mantra.

5. Akal Ustat

Waho Akal Ki Ustat, Jo Tum Akhand Path Kare

Meaning: "Hail to the Praise of the Eternal One, He who recites the Eternal Word."

Akal Ustat is a potent mantra from the Sikh tradition and has been used for centuries to bring about deep spiritual healing. It was designed to call upon the divine energy of the universe, and its resonance is said to activate all seven chakras. This mantra invokes the divine teacher to uplift our consciousness, fill us with courage, and help us find inspiration in difficult times. Akal Ustat is believed to purify the karmic field and all of our subtle bodies and is an incredibly powerful tool for Kundalini yoga practitioners. When chanted out loud, Akal Ustat can bring about deep relaxation and inner peace while also calming the mind and aiding in meditation practice. As such, it is a wonderful resource for your Kundalini yoga practice.

The power of mantras and mudras is undeniable. While both have been used for centuries to bring about personal transformation, they are only fully realized when used in conjunction with regular Kundalini yoga and meditation practice. With a deeper understanding of the energetics behind each mudra and mantra, practitioners can gain insight into the unique gifts and capabilities of each, allowing them to more fully realize the potential within their practice. As one begins to explore the vast potential of Kundalini yoga and meditation, these mudras and mantras can be used as powerful tools to bring about transformation and spiritual awakening!

Chapter 6: How to Do Kundalini Meditation

Kundalini meditation is a powerful way to access spiritual power and energy within yourself. With practice and dedication, one can awaken the Kundalini energy, known as the "serpent power," which exists at the base of the spine. This powerful energy replaces negative thoughts and creates an immense sense of joy and spiritual balance when accessed. By combining ancient yoga techniques with relaxing breathwork and visualization, Kundalini meditation uncovers our ultimate potential, both spiritually and mentally. Through this yogic practice, we search deeply into our souls for healing, strength, courage, self-awareness, and inner peace.

Kundalini meditation allows us to clear our minds, relax our bodies, quieten inner chatter, connect with our spirit guides, and come closer to whichever higher power we believe in. This chapter will explain what Kundalini meditation is and its benefits, the step-by-step instructions on practicing it, and provide some tips on how to enhance it. Ultimately, with consistency and dedication, Kundalini meditation can help to create a better connection to the divine and yourself.

What Is Kundalini Meditation?

Kundalini meditation is revolutionizing the way people approach spirituality and self-development. Through a combination of deep breathing techniques, yoga postures, mantras, and visualizations, Kundalini meditation brings a spiritual element to a physical practice.

Primarily focusing on channeling energy that rises from the base of the spine up through the body, these meditations bring mental and physical balance. With so many different combinations available, Kundalini meditation can be tailored to fit anyone's needs. Whether someone wants to focus on internal dialogue or work on manifesting desired outcomes in their life, there is a Kundalini meditation for each stage of personal transformation.

Benefits of Kundalini Meditation

Kundalini meditation helps practitioners to access the universal energy within themselves and bring the body, mind, and spirit into alignment. Many followers who practice it find that it brings many benefits, such as improved physical and mental health, greater spiritual development, enhanced creativity and intuition, improved clarity of thought, and better concentration and focus. Furthermore, as it encourages a more centered lifestyle, practitioners of Kundalini often report feeling more connected to themselves and the wider world. In essence, Kundalini meditation is a path toward understanding one's true purpose in life.

1. Increase Creativity

This powerful practice promotes creativity, agility of the mind, and emotional stability. It unlocks suppressed creative energy and aids in tapping into one's creative potential. Through regular Kundalini meditation, you'll find that you have increased focus and clarity of thought, can create inspirational ideas, and foster a positive emotional state. Kundalini meditation also creates the perfect ambiance for self-reflection and spiritual growth, which helps us connect with our intuition and access the unconscious part of ourselves. As a result, we can discern what truly inspires us, expand upon our current thought processes, and become more original in our concept creation. Ultimately, Kundalini Meditation helps open the pathway towards finding multiple ways of creativity that reflect our selves.

2. Balancing the Nervous System

Kundalini meditation is gaining traction as a technique to naturally balance the nervous system. Through its emphasis on patience, focus, and understanding, Kundalini meditation creates an equilibrium between mind and body. When practiced regularly, this technique can help individuals cultivate inner peace and better manage their emotions. It can also serve to lower stress levels as well as reduce anxiety. As a result of these effects, practitioners will often face life's obstacles with ease by better managing both physical and mental health.

3. Enhancing Intuition

Through the growth and expansion that this inner spiritual power brings, practitioners can dramatically enhance their intuition. Those who use Kundalini meditation have improved cognitive abilities and a greater sense of insight. This results in better decision-making processes, more creative problem-solving skills, and heightened awareness of environments. Thus, it gives users a more holistic understanding of their existence and reality, helping them gain an otherworldly perspective on life's matters. By strengthening intuition, we can clearly understand our purpose in life and be guided towards becoming contented individuals.

4. Improves Mental Clarity

Meditating through Kundalini is a forceful method of improving mental clarity. While many studies have proven the benefits of meditation, it is especially powerful when combined with moving postures and breathing exercises, which start to activate and balance energetic pathways in the body. Practicing Kundalini meditation frees any mental blocks formed from stress and anxiety, giving you a greater perspective and ability better solve tough problems. Regular practice helps foster clarity, creativity, and concentration skills, which can improve decision-making capabilities for daily life, whether on a personal or professional level.

5. Stimulates Better Sleep

Practicing Kundalini meditation can be a great way to relax and recharge to get a better night's sleep. When you meditate, you breathe deeply, which relaxes your body and slows down the heart rate. This can help our brains transition more quickly from the day's stress into a restful sleep state. In addition, Kundalini meditation enables us to explore our emotions and process them healthily, leaving us calm and encouraging better sleep. Releasing built-up tension helps us fall asleep faster, stay asleep longer, and wake up feeling energized. These benefits make it clear that taking time out of your day for a Kundalini meditation session can be essential for getting a better night's sleep.

6. Reduces Stress and Anxiety

This ancient form of Indian meditation brings the ability to reduce stress and anxiety through breathwork, chanting mantras, movements, and visualization to connect deeply with oneself. Kundalini meditation creates feelings of relaxation by releasing endorphins that reduce cortisol levels and decrease anxiety. The movement component encourages people to release any negative emotions they're holding onto while increasing their self-awareness. Kundalini meditation not only aids in reducing stress but reduces physical symptoms such as headaches and back pain. This meditation helps people stay more present in the moment while being mindful of their thoughts and feelings, enabling them to live life with greater fulfillment, peace, and satisfaction.

7. Clears the Subconscious Mind

Kundalini meditation has been practiced for thousands of years and is said to be the work of the gods, providing a path to enlightening the minds of mere mortals. It combines intention, sound, and breath as a discipline to clear the subconscious mind. Long-term practitioners swear that Kundalini meditation opens them up to possibilities not accessible before, from increased creativity and mental clarity to greater self-confidence. Consequently, they tap into their deepest meditative space at will, resulting in profound insights and personal breakthroughs that can revolutionize their lives. Ultimately, clearing our subconscious through Kundalini meditation enables us to unveil the blueprint of ourselves with newfound clarity and purpose.

8. Fosters Self-Awareness

Over time, this meditative practice also fosters self-awareness. People who practice it can observe the changes occurring within their inner consciousness. This leads to a greater understanding of one's self, which can be a wonderful journey of growth and understanding. As an individual becomes increasingly aware of their inner workings and gains insight into their behavior and its effects on the world around them, they can make decisions that improve both their life and the lives of those they share it with. Therefore, Kundalini meditation is truly a valuable gift by promoting self-awareness and the overall health of body and mind.

9. Regulates Emotions

Practicing Kundalini can help one better understand oneself, that is, a better understanding of our physical sensations and emotions. With this knowledge, it becomes easier to identify, understand and process negative feelings without letting them take control. The mental clarity achieved by Kundalini allows for a perspective that can help calm the mind and gain control over erratic thoughts or compulsions. It effectively cultivates patience, understanding, acceptance of oneself, and increased emotional stability, leading to better relationships. In other words, a regular

Kundalini practice promotes mindfulness of feelings and intelligent responses that are beneficial for everyone involved.

10. Improved Overall Health

Regular meditation practice can improve physical, mental, and emotional well-being as the mind becomes calmer, stress levels lower, and self-confidence increases. People who have adopted it into their routine have reported having better cognitive functions and improved responses to inflammation-related diseases such as arthritis and lupus. Practicing Kundalini also releases energy from various parts of the brain, resulting in improved overall health. It enables a person to stay motivated and proactive while setting goals and working towards achieving them. Therefore, this form of meditation can help anyone to create an overall healthy lifestyle that promotes long-term wellness.

Step-by-Step Instructions for Kundalini Meditation

It is surprisingly simple to get started, but like most good things in life, it does require commitment and dedication to foster its full potential. By setting aside time each day for practice, you can enjoy the countless benefits of this ancient practice, from improved emotional clarity and enhanced self-awareness to heightened intuition and spiritual presence. A synthesizing of breath work, mantras, and postures with awareness toward inner wisdom creates an enriching experience that encourages holistic transformation both inwards and outwards. Here are the basic steps to get started:

1. Set the Intention

Setting an intention for your Kundalini meditation can help you focus on your goals and bring more clarity to your practice. Start by quieting your mind and taking a few deep breaths. Finally, take some time to self-reflect with an open heart and mind, to determine what you want to get out of the meditation. Determine how you want to grow from the experience and set clear intentions regarding what you aim for spiritually, mentally, emotionally, or physically. Be specific about why your intention matters for where you want to go in life. With a strong foundation in place and positive affirmations added to the mix, a Kundalini meditation immersed with intention can reshape your mindset and alter your perspective. Through this powerful practice, experience a deeper connection between yourself and the cosmic realm.

2. Choose a Meditation Posture

When choosing a meditation posture, choose one that supports your body and allows you to be comfortable for an extended period. Traditionally, this is done in a seated position, such as on the floor, cushion, or chair. Suppose any physical limitations make it difficult for you to sit for long periods. In that case, there are lying postures used in Kundalini meditation as well. The most vital thing is to find the posture that allows your back and neck to be evenly supported so that your muscles don't tire out during the meditation. Whichever posture you choose will help set the foundation for peace and stillness while opening yourself up to Kundalini energy within your body.

3. Focus on Your Breath

Focusing on your breath while meditating with Kundalini techniques will reduce stress and psychological trauma while also connecting you with your spiritual or higher self effectively. When focusing on your breath during Kundalini meditation, be mindful of the depth and length of each inhalation and exhalation. This mindfulness allows practitioners to create a reflective space within themselves, giving them access to their truest potential by awakening their inner energies. With practice, any individual can profoundly connect with Kundalini energy through mindful breathing during Kundalini meditation.

4. Connect to the Divine

By connecting ourselves to the divine, we can go beyond our everyday thoughts and into a state of knowledge, understanding, and peace that can be difficult to find in our chaotic modern lives. We can access this special level of awareness through Kundalini meditation, chanting mantras, and focusing on certain body parts to create more balance in our energy flow. Once we connect with the divine, it gives us the courage to take on whatever challenge we may face and the capacity for great inner peace. Whether searching for a way to reduce anxiety or seek spiritual growth, connecting to the divine through Kundalini meditation will give you a strong foundation to begin your journey.

5. Do Not Force Meditation

Kundalini meditation should never be forced. Different people will experience this form of meditation in distinct and unique ways, so it's crucial to remain open-minded and not expect a particular outcome. As practitioners become more experienced with the technique, they are likely to further develop their skills and refine the meditation process as needed. It is essential to give your body and mind time to adjust during each session, as some forms of Kundalini can be very intense. Only practice with a teacher with experience and knowledge about such an intricate form of meditation. When done correctly, this meditation can become incredibly powerful and move energy through your chakras like no other.

6. Use Mantras and Mudras

Finding inner peace and balance can be challenging for many in today's hectic and often stressful world. Kundalini meditation can be an effective tool in helping us reach this tranquility. Using mantras and mudras will deepen one's experience and lead to profound transformation. Mantras are chanting sounds that help increase our awareness, while mudras involve specific hand gestures to focus the mind, aid concentration, and bring greater clarity. Combined with traditional yoga postures, they produce an even greater effect, encouraging the mind and body to open up more deeply and cultivate a serene atmosphere conducive to achieving lasting balance.

7. End Your Session with Gratitude

One way to ensure you make the most of Kundalini meditation is to end your session with gratitude. Consider what this unique experience has given you, perhaps a feeling of peace or insight about yourself, and be thankful for it. Allow gratitude to permeate your mind and body as you close off the meditation session, carrying positive energy into your daily life. The more you practice, the more consistent and powerful its effects can become. The key is to remain open and willing to experience something new each time you practice Kundalini meditation.

Tips for Enhancing Your Kundalini Meditation Experience

Uncovering an intensified sense of tranquility and awareness through a Kundalini meditation practice can be incredibly rewarding. With practice, anyone can use it to detach from worldly worries and gain insight into their innermost thoughts and emotions. Being open-minded and focused on the practice, not just during meditation sessions but through daily life, will be the most beneficial way to make progress with this form of meditation. Here are some tips to help you get the most out of your Kundalini meditation experience.

1. Create a Sacred Space

Creating a sacred space for Kundalini meditation is an excellent way to enhance your experience and get the most out of practice. This could involve bringing in elements and items such as incense, calming music, candles, yoga chairs or bolsters, essential oils, and more. Doing this in advance will help you relax into your Kundalini session, improving focus and attention while encouraging a deeper state of tranquility. Incorporating personal objects such as photos or totems can also be beneficial in helping to create a comfortable atmosphere that resonates with your spiritual needs. Ultimately, having this dedicated space that allows you to pause and reflect without distraction is key to cultivating a positive journey through Kundalini meditation.

2. Wear Comfortable Clothing

To get the most out of a deep, spiritual experience, wear comfortable and unrestricted clothing. Clothing should also provide some coverage if lying on the ground, as particular revealing postures may be called for during Kundalini meditation. Opting for loose, breathable fabrics such as organic cotton or hemp and layered pieces that can be easily added or removed are great choices when exploring Kundalini meditation. Making sure comfort comes first will allow meditators to stay focused on the many mental and spiritual benefits of this life-transforming experience.

3. Practice at the Same Time Every Day

Regular and consistent Kundalini practice is one of the most crucial aspects of enhancing your meditation experience. Practicing at the same time every day will give you structure, stability, and quality to your meditations. When your body learns the daily habit, it eventually enters into a trance-like state of meditation more easily and quickly. When practiced in a relaxed fashion at the same time each day, you build momentum for deeper concentration levels and an enhanced transformation through connection with spirit. Establishing a Kundalini practice as part of a daily routine helps promote emotional well-being for those seeking peace, healing, and joy.

4. Incorporate Essential Oils

Incorporating essential oils while practicing Kundalini meditation can be a lovely, serene way to enhance your experience. Essential oils have been used for centuries in spiritual and healing ceremonies, and their aromatic properties can influence your intention and mental focus. They can also open up the body's chakra centers which are key for unlocking

Kundalini energy. Start by adding a few drops of essential oils such as Frankincense, Lavender, or Basil to a diffuser, or use them topically by applying them around the heart, throat, and lower brow areas with light massage strokes. Discover how essential oils can transport you into deeper states of meditation and expand your connection to the spiritual world.

5. Visualize a Goal

With the right visualizations and imagery, you can improve your experience. Having a clear picture of what you want to achieve through meditation can help you stay focused during practice and create deeper relaxation within yourself. By visualizing the outcome you want from your meditation journey, whether feeling calm, connected to nature, or released from stress, your mind will be even more attuned to the effects of breathing meditations, mantras, and other spiritual exercises. Acknowledging desired outcomes during a session can put you in control of your path toward realization. Anchor yourself to the goal so your journey is more successful with each practice.

6. Journal Reflections

Enhancing your Kundalini meditation experience can be difficult. However, journaling reflections on your meditation practice can help you to quantify and track improvements. Reflecting on the time spent in meditation allows you to better comprehend the sensations experienced and augment your understanding of what is occurring during the practice. It can act as a motivator to deepen and continue your practice and reveal where modifications may be required. Regular journaling allows one to connect with inner truths and unlock new spiritual realms that are otherwise inaccessible.

7. Practice Meditation in Nature

Many people don't realize that the environment in which you practice meditation has a lot to do with the positive effects they can experience. Kundalini meditation done in nature can be particularly enhanced because of the natural energy present in outdoor environments. Practicing outside lets practitioners connect directly with their inner selves and benefit from Mother Nature's healing energy. Exposure to fresh air, sunshine, plants, and animals can also have many physiological benefits, including improved immune systems and reduced fatigue. So, for those looking to take their meditation practice up a notch, being at one with nature is worth considering.

Kundalini Meditation is an ancient practice that has the potential to bring about great transformation and healing in those who are willing to commit to its practice. Through regular practice, one can experience profound spiritual transformation and unlock your full potential. You can take your Kundalini meditation practice to the next level with simple tips, such as incorporating essential oils, visualizing a goal, journaling reflections, and practicing in nature. With consistent effort and dedication, anyone can experience the potential benefits of this powerful meditative practice.

Chapter 7: Arambha: A Root Awakening

As we progress along the serpent's path of spiritual awakening, we can observe the Kundalini energy rise to open and clear each of the many chakras that line our spines. This is an often compared process with much symbolism and strength embedded within it. The term "Kundalini" can also be translated to mean "the curl of the lock of hair of the beloved" and represents the creative power in all consciousness. A thorough understanding of this transformational journey is full of revelations that take us to deeper places within ourselves, bringing awareness to both new possibilities as well as ancient truths.

This chapter of the Kundalini Yoga Guide introduces and guides you through the first stage of Kundalini awakening, Arambha. Here, we will discuss what happens during this stage, which chakras are affected, how they can affect your life, and the untied knots. We will then present simple step-by-step instructions for a few kriyas and sequences that target the stimulation of this stage, as well as some balancing postures and pranayama practices to support this process. Finally, we will close with a few meditations to integrate this whole experience.

The First Stage of Kundalini Awakening

Arambha, or the first stage of the Kundalini awakening process, is a deeply emotional and transformative experience. This initial phase is miraculous, as it sets a life-altering introspective journey in motion. On an energetic level, it begins a purification process and re-adjustment of subtle energies within the body. During Arambha, a person may feel a penetrating heat come through their body as if their chi was being awakened from its dormant state. As this wave of energy builds, physical pain can be experienced as tensions are released from deep within our body. During this stage, it is essential to maintain balance and not overextend oneself beyond what is comfortable. The practice of self-love and non-attachment can often provide support for navigating through this profound journey to find joy in sacred metamorphosis.

A. What Happens during Arambha

Arambha is the first stage of the Kundalini awakening process and involves a process of profound transformation. The innermost energies lying dormant in an individual are woken due to increased spiritual activity. The power of this exchange releases energetic blockages within the body, allowing pure, unconditional love to lift one beyond limitations into higher states of consciousness. Several phenomena often occur during Arambha, such as intuitive knowledge or altered states of mental, emotional, and physical awareness. In some cases, even psychic abilities such as clairvoyance or healing powers can come into play. Arambha is an incredibly transformative experience that allows one to journey sublimely toward cosmic consciousness.

B. Chakras Affected and Their Effects

Our chakras are affected during Arambha (the first stage of Kundalini awakening). Each of the seven main chakras is activated, energized, and balanced as we progress on this spiritual journey. Our root chakra is connected to a sense of security and being grounded. As it heals and opens, we begin to feel more secure within ourselves and connect more deeply with the physical world around us. Our sacral chakra deals with our emotional intelligence, sensuality, and creativity and helps us become aware of our life's purpose. Healing this chakra increases intuition and caring towards self and others while lessening any attachments that may have held us back from achieving our true potential.

All the chakras are influenced during Arambha.

Our solar plexus holds much of our motivations, determination, power, influence over others, and even personal identity. Mental clarity increases when energy starts flowing here again, allowing for strong trust in one's decisions. This can be a powerful motivator for doing things we want to do or that our soul craves for itself in terms of increasing spirituality. All in all, these aroused energies work together to holistically rejuvenate each aspect of day-to-day life, from physical well-being to emotional stability.

C. Untying of the Knots

Many yogic and spiritual concepts create the idea of knots or symbolic errors in the brain's functions that hinder us from understanding our true nature. "Untying of the knots" is a metaphor for enlightenment related to the Kundalini awakening's first stage. In this step, we learn to foster an awareness of what has been hindering us from reconnecting with the primal self which resides deep within our souls. It teaches us how to identify and discard any karma, emotional baggage, or patterns that block us from living life more consciously. By loosening our attachment to all things mental and external, we can tap into inner strength and knowledge, providing liberation through self-illumination. As one reaches Arambha and begins untying their knots, they are devoting themselves to a profound spiritual journey toward every individual's highest truth.

Kriyas and Sequences

One crucial aspect to consider during Arambha is kriyas and sequences. Kriyas are physical movements that can be performed in rhythm or gracefully, depending on the person's preference. They can range from simple rhythmic arm movements to more complicated dance-like body movements. While executing the kriya, one should be conscious of how their breath connects to it and how it affects their overall well-being. Sequences also bring clarity and focus to a practitioner's practice by helping them become more mindful of subtle aspects of their physical practice, such as breathing, calming down of thoughts, and postures. Kriyas and sequences during Arambha play an integral part in facilitating an individual's journey towards Kundalini Awakening.

A. Simple Breathwork-Based Kriya Using Pranayama

Whether you are a beginner or an experienced yogi, simple breathwork-based kriya using pranayama during the first stage of Kundalini awakening can take your practice to the next level. Pranayama is the ancient yogic practice of regulating your breath and increasing prana, which is often referred to as the life force in yoga. Combining pranayama with guided meditation can center your mind and body into a state of higher consciousness so you can tap into the power of Kundalini and experience its healing benefits. Practicing regular kriya during Arambha will assist with developing new levels of mental clarity, self-awareness, and spiritual insight, which can be carried over into all areas of life and bring greater personal growth.

B. Chakra-Activating Sequence with Mantra

A chakra-activating sequence coupled with a mantra is an excellent strategy to maximize the potential of the Arambha stage and keep energy from becoming blocked. During this exercise, you focus on each chakra while visualizing the energies and repeating affirmations to open up your energy centers and create a smooth, balanced flow of universal energy throughout your body. Not only will this technique help you tap into the potential of your Kundalini awakening better, but it can also give you a greater understanding of your center power and offer spiritual guidance as you progress through all stages of awakening.

C. Kundalini Mudra to Activate the Serpent Power

Practicing Kundalini Mudra is an ancient Indian tantric practice designed to awaken the Kundalini energy. Hence, it is used to activate the serpent power during Arambha. It involves the use of hand and body postures, together with a specific breathing technique. Regularly performing this practice can raise their vibrations and energies that eventually cause enlightenment. This meditation practice enables one to achieve awareness of their inner divinity and allows them to better understand their potential. This creates a sense of balance in life which increases vitality and well-being. Practitioners often claim that they experience an increased insight into a deeper understanding of themselves, coupled with a heightened internal connection. Overall, practicing Kundalini Mudra provides physical and spiritual benefits essential for living a healthy life.

Balancing Asanas

One of the most significant parts of Arambha is learning how to include asanas in your practice to promote stillness, grounding, and focus. Balancing asanas uses the concept of counterbalances to find stability both physically and mentally. As practitioners become more comfortable with each pose, they can learn to be mindful and stable while stretching the body's boundaries. Remember that all practices should be tailored specifically for each individual. Balancing asanas should be performed gently and with respect for yourself and your abilities. Arambha can bring you closer to finding harmony within yourself and embracing alignment between your mind, body, and soul.

1. Sun Salutations for Balancing and Renewal

Arambha is the perfect time to reset and recharge, as well as look inward and find balance. Sun salutations are a great way of achieving balanced renewal during this time. This popular yoga practice is traditionally performed at sunrise or right before engaging in any strenuous physical activity. This practice allows us to center ourselves and become re-aligned with our true intention so we feel deeply renewed and balanced. These salutations strengthen our bodies while we are deeply connected with each breath, helping us focus on mental and physical progressive improvement. They involve mantras that serve to both reinvigorate and further calm the mind from all our daily stresses.

2. Corpse Pose to Center and Balance the Mind

The corpse pose is an important position used to center and balance the mind by yoga practitioners of all levels. It is a time to pause during practice and become mindful of present sensations occurring in the body. Many people find the corpse pose to be one of the most difficult postures because it requires total stillness for an extended period. One must make a conscious effort to relax every muscle group, from head to toe, releasing tension from both mind and body. When this posture is practiced correctly, it provides clarity, aids in healing on physical and emotional levels, and brings understanding about how energy naturally flows through the body. Corpse pose is often used at the beginning and end of yoga classes but can work wonders if we dedicate more attention to it, even just five minutes when necessary throughout the day, to re-center and balance the mind that so easily succumbs to stressors in our lives.

3. Seated Poses for Releasing Tension

Before starting any yoga session, take a moment for relaxation and release any built-up tension. Seated poses are some of the best poses for doing this at the start of your practice. In seated poses such as Baddhakonasana (The Cobbler Pose) and Vajrasana (The Thunderbolt Pose), you can gently open up the hips and relax your abdominal muscles. You can also use props such as blocks or blankets to make the posture more comfortable if you're stiff in the hip area. Taking conscious deep breaths while in these poses can further relax your body, improving your ability to move into other poses more effectively. When you are focusing on releasing physical tension, setting an intention also helps you stay focused on that goal during Arambha.

4. Inversions to Connect with the Inner Self

Arambha is a practice that can be seen as an invitation to connect with our inner self and grow through accepting the change. Inversions are essential to this practice, as they can bring about a deeper understanding of oneself and allow for work on any challenging emotions that may arise. Inverting the body is a powerful way to bring about clarity and centering, ultimately allowing us to transform how we experience each moment, create mindful intention and manifest greater joy in our lives. With regular practice, inversions can become an ever-expanding process of connection and liberation within ourselves.

5. Spinal Twists to Rebalance the Chakras

Spinal twists can be performed at the beginning of an Arambha to re-balance your chakras. Starting at the sacrum area, twist your upper body, keeping your hips and pelvis facing forward. This will bring awareness to the powers underlying, supporting, and nourishing you from the ground up. Move up through the vertebrae, twisting through each segment until you reach the C6. Feel the openness between each spinal segment as it moves with grace in a fluid motion. As you twist more deeply into each movement, merging breath with spiritual source energy to connect deeper within, there will be moments where this connection is palpable. Shift mental awareness to focus on that opening and expansiveness while harnessing that power into your physical form. The energy flow has been re-balanced. You stand ready to start your day anew.

Pranayama Practices for Kundalini Activation

Pranayama practices are often recommended for those looking to activate their Kundalini energy. Pranayama is a type of yoga focused on breathing, and since the breath is the cosmic energy that sustains life, it's only natural that using specific breathing techniques to access inner, dormant energy can be beneficial. When practiced regularly, pranayama can help one become more sensitive to their subtle energy fields, such as their chakras, which are thought to be responsible for Kundalini activation. Furthermore, slow and conscious deep breaths calm the mind while releasing toxins from the body. This clears up obstacles that prohibit Kundalini activation.

1. Rhythmic Breathing for Inner Connection

Arambha, the start of something new, can be made even more powerful with some rhythmic breathing. Taking just 10 or 15 seconds to take a deep breath and slowly exhale will allow your body to connect internally with the part of it that is ready for change. This inner connection will bring forth strength and focus, helping you accomplish previously impossible goals. Tune into yourself via rhythmic breathing as you begin this new journey and reap the rewards.

2. Ujjayi Pranayama to Open the Throat Chakra

Ujjayi pranayama is a great way to open the throat chakra during Arambha. This yoga breathing technique involves a low, steady inhalation and exhalation that flows from the center of the chest. It promotes relaxation, removes energy stagnation in the body, and clears residual tension and blocks in the body and mind. The sound generated in Ujjayi pranayama that comes from deep within your throat helps you relax while practicing Arambha while strengthening your cardiovascular system, and aiding with clear communication and problem-solving. Since this type of breathing focuses on awareness of breath flow, it encourages harmony between respiration and physical movement throughout each iteration. Thus, Ujjayi Pranayama can be very helpful in opening up the throat chakra during Arambha, helping us to balance fearlessness in speaking our truth with the vulnerability that it requires.

3. Bhastrika to Stimulate the Nervous System

Executing Bhastrika pranayama is an effective way to stimulate the nervous system. This ancient practice of rhythmic breathing increases oxygen levels, boosts energy, and calms the mind and body. During Bhastrika, your inhalation and exhalation cycle should be done with intention and concentration as they are used to send healing energy throughout the body. It's beneficial when practiced slowly during Arambha because it has a calming effect that relaxes tense muscles so that you can enjoy all of the benefits of the sessions. This practice can also remove toxins from your internal organs while cleansing your bloodstream. Making Bhastrika part of your Kundalini meditation routine is a wonderful way to better receive its therapeutic effects!

4. Sitali Pranayama to Calm the Mind

Sitali Pranayama is a helpful and calming exercise that can be used during the beginning stages of yoga. Sitali Pranayama begins with deep inhales and exhales, curling your tongue and gently rolling and unrolling it while breathing through it. Another part of this exercise is to then take sips from the curled tongue as if drinking water from a spoon or trying to imitate slurping something up. This exercise opens and calms the body, improving other practices such as meditation. It sends a message to both physical and mental states that all is safe in the environment, so there is no need for alarm or worries about external disturbances. Altogether, it imparts a sense of clarity and balance, making it incredibly useful during Arambha when trying to achieve a meditative state or disengage from tension and stress that may exist in the present moment.

5. Brahmari Pranayama for Deep Relaxation

Arambha can be a stressful time for many practitioners of yoga, especially those just starting. That's why deep relaxation is so critical during this period. One beneficial practice to employ is Brahmari Pranayama, or humming bee breath. This breathing exercise quiets the mind and brings mindful awareness to the breath. It also has numerous health benefits, such as lowering stress levels, encouraging better sleep patterns, and calming the central nervous system. The humming sound created during the practice can be incredibly soothing and create a sense of stillness in the body and mind. Regularly practicing Brahmari Pranayama during Arambha can cultivate greater peace, tranquility, and deep relaxation through all stages of their yoga journey.

Closing the Practice

As you come to the end of your practice, allow yourself a few moments to reflect on what you have achieved during your session. Let any emotions or feelings surface, and take note of them without judgment. Notice how you feel physically and mentally, and give thanks for the lessons learned throughout this journey. Spend the last few minutes in stillness, allowing the practice to settle fully, and then slowly open your eyes.

At this point, you have successfully initiated the first stage of Kundalini awakening, Arambha! Through a combination of breathing exercises, pranayama methods, and restorative yoga postures, you have begun the journey toward spiritual growth and self-awareness. With regular practice of these techniques, you can continue to open and develop the chakras triggered during your journey.

The knowledge and insights gained throughout the process are invaluable tools in your spiritual growth, so take time to reflect on all that you have learned. Enjoy this newfound awareness and continue to explore the depths of your inner universe as you journey along the path of Kundalini yoga. Namaste!

Chapter 8: Ghata: Unlocking the Heart Chakra

The next stage in the Kundalini yoga journey is called Ghata, or "the cleansing stage." This phase follows Arambha and is a crucial step towards further spiritual growth. During this stage, practitioners take on an attitude of receiving vast amounts of transformation and healing on all levels to enter their bodies. Completion of the Ghata phase requires patience, dedication, courage, and above all else, an open heart and mind. With these in place, you'll find unity within yourself and your surroundings and the courage to keep exploring the spiritual path.

This chapter will provide an overview of the various aspects of Ghata and how to use Kundalini yoga to reach this stage. It will explain what happens during Ghata, the chakras affected and their effects, and the kriyas and sequences for reaching this stage. Asanas and pranayama practices for Ghata will also be discussed, as well as how to close the practice. The information in this chapter is meant to be an introduction and a general understanding of the Ghata phase.

Ghata: The Cleansing Stage

The ancient practice of Kundalini awakening has been slowly gaining popularity in modern-day spiritual circles. The cleansing stage of this process, often called Ghata, is an essential step in awakening your internal wisdom and power. Ghata is all about purifying the body and mind to prepare for the ascension of energy taking place within the body. This includes deep breathing exercises, chanting mantras, clearing the mind of any negative thoughts, and visualization exercises. Once the cleansing phase has been completed, the journey toward spiritual strength can truly begin. Ghata is vital in awakening your Kundalini energy and should not be missed on many paths to enlightenment.

A. What Happens during Ghata

Kundalini energy begins to rise through the seven chakras, and old beliefs and unhealthy habits are cleared away as it progresses. This can cause various physical and mental effects, from tingling sensations throughout the body to waves of intense emotion. People often experience heightened self-awareness during this time, allowing for deeper insight into their thoughts and feelings. Although Ghata can be uncomfortable at first, working through it with mindful awareness provides great clarity and insight – a key element on the path of spiritual growth.

B. Chakras Affected and Their Effects

Ghata, or the cleansing stage of Kundalini awakening, can affect each of the seven chakras throughout the body. The root chakra, at the base of the spine, is cleansed to open us up to abundant energy and support. The sacral chakra is cleared for emotional openness and proper creative flow. The solar plexus chakra is purified to allow us unyielding confidence and determination.

The heart chakra is enlightened to create powerful love and empathy within us. The throat chakra is opened, increasing communication and honest self-expression. Lastly, the third eye chakra gains clarity generating greater intuition along with sharper mental focus, while the crown chakra becomes more connected to the divine, allowing spiritual awakening. During Ghata, all of the chakras are affected, creating balance within and manifesting great growth and wisdom within us.

C. Untying of the Knots

Dissolving the knots of energy through Ghata is a critical process in activating Kundalini. It creates a ripple effect throughout the body and soul, making our natural energy flow substantially uncongested. This can create a powerful sense of awareness and clarity, as chakras may respond in a way that was not previously possible. The kriyas or practices used during this stage gradually uncoil these tightly knotted energies to further awaken consciousness on a higher level. This can benefit various aspects of life, such as emotional balancing, physical well-being, and spiritual growth. Furthermore, it unlocks your full potential so you can take your true path toward fulfillment more clearly and vigorously.

Kriyas and Sequences for the Ghata Stage

In yoga, the Ghata stage is a strength-building portion of practice that focuses on activating and integrating body systems. A few of the great tools for this work are kriyas and sequences. *Kriyas* involve extending postures with repetitions or alternating sequences. These sequences put poses together in a way that gives rise to ever-deepening layers of experience as you move through them, from a physical challenge into full mental/physical integration. With regular practice of kriyas and sequences, we can develop flexibility, strength, endurance, and focus that help us move beyond the boundaries of our current level of ability into something entirely new.

1. Uddiyana Bandha

Yoga practitioners often use Uddiyana Bandha to remove physical tension and tightness while mental blocks are cleared away. Generally achieved in the standing position, Uddiyana Bandha is the practice of sucking the navel area inward towards the spine. This "engaging" of our bodies creates a sudden rush of energy, balancing the flow within us and facilitating further cleansing during Kundalini awakening. It also builds internal heat and reduces stress in the abdominal area while controlling our breath through conscious inhalation and exhalation. The practice cleanses our systems more thoroughly during Ghata, allowing for an even stronger connection to our highest selves when we reach the next stage in Kundalini awakening.

2. Nauli

Nauli Kriya is a powerful cleansing ritual commonly practiced in the Ghata stage of the Kundalini awakening. It works to expel stagnant energy and toxins within the body, simultaneously encouraging new vitality. Through abdominal muscle contractions, practitioners can strengthen their core and sacral chakras, allowing energy to move freely through the system. This encourages clarity in the physical body and is a gateway to deeper levels of self-awareness. Nauli kriya offers both liberation and transformation as participants get to know themselves more deeply, sparking immense healing on a spiritual level.

3. Agni Sara

Ghata, the cleansing stage of the Kundalini awakening, can often be an energy-consuming process. To help revitalize your energy and quicken the cleansing process, many practitioners have turned to Agni Sara Kriya. This energizing pranayama exercise cleanses the internal organs while working the core abdominal muscles, stimulating the manifestation of Kundalini energy. It's commonly recommended as a great practice to accompany any sort of Kundalini work or meditation you may be undertaking. Ultimately, Agni Sara Kriya is a wonderful tool for anyone looking to maximize their Ghata practice and further activate their full spiritual potential.

4. Kumbhaka

Kumbhaka kriya is a powerful meditation practice aimed at clearing out any energetic blockages in the body, allowing for an open channel and better flow of life force energy. During this stage, focus on the energy centers within you while holding your breath. You also focus on prana, or life force, and aim to bring fresh and vital energy into your being that helps create mental clarity, spiritual connection, and improved overall well-being. Practitioners usually begin with shorter periods of breath holds to gain mastery over it before attempting longer breaths with practice and dedication. The goal is to take long breaths without feeling uncomfortable and eventually progress into even deeper states of pranayama, which brings greater clarity and presence.

5. Kapalabhati

The Kapalabhati technique enables one to fine-tune their prana, or vital life-force energy, throughout their body. This work is done through a special type of breathing known as Kapalabhati pranayama. Also called "shining skull breath," it clears out toxins from the organism and balances energies within the body. As this process happens, your physical and spiritual well-being will start to improve and release blockages along all energy pathways, allowing for a powerful Kundalini awakening. With continued practice, you'll feel spiritually invigorated with each inhalation and exhalation of breath, connecting you to the divine source within you.

Asanas for Ghata

Asanas are a series of postures and breathing exercises also designed to cleanse the mind and body. This stage is the start of a journey towards union with source energy. Each asana detoxifies us at the physical and energetic level, gently pushing our minds and bodies into harmony so that we can move through each blockage in our transformation process. Moving through this self-nurturing practice calms the nervous system and strengthens both mental clarity and emotional resilience. After completing these exercises, practitioners often feel energized, peaceful, and deeply centered in themselves. Ghata focuses on creating a balance between movement and stillness so that you feel restored to your true state of being, an elevated connection to the divine energy that brings more happiness to life's difficult moments.

1. Ustrasana

Ustrasana is a demanding asana that focuses on releasing stagnant energy involuntarily stored in your body associated with unresolved memories, suppressed emotions, and trauma. This asana is performed by lying on your back, bending the knee, and bringing it close to your chest while lifting the hips and extending the arms upwards. Ustrasana is a powerful exercise that helps clear out any blockages in our energetic pathways, allowing for more peaceful energy to flow through us.

In addition to the energetic cleanse, Ustrasana provides the physical strength gained from the deep stretching and strengthening within postures like this one that strengthens us physically and mentally for facing future challenges. For those looking to unlock the transformative power of Kundalini yoga, Ustrasana for Ghata can be a foundational pillar of practice in a customized program.

2. Bhujangasana

Practicing Bhujangasana or "Cobra Pose" is an excellent way to begin the Ghata stage. This pose awakens and energizes the spine while opening up blocked energy along the spine. It encourages the full expansion of breath in the body, allowing one to elevate your consciousness. To enter the posture, lie on your stomach and then slowly lift your chest off the floor while arching your back and keeping your legs on the ground.

The cobra pose will help open up any blocked energy along the spine, allowing a more free-flowing flow of prana throughout the body. With an open and clear mind, Bhujangasana can also effectively purify old emotions that no longer serve you, making way for new energies to emerge. In sum, if you are starting your own Kundalini awakening journey, don't forget to make Bhujangasana your companion!

3. Adho Mukha Svanasana

If you want to improve your overall health and connect with your Kundalini energy, Adho Mukha Svanasana is a great place to start. Also known as the Downward-Facing Dog Pose, this powerful combination of stretching and breathing can help accelerate the cleansing stage in Kundalini awakening. To perform this pose, start on all fours and slowly press your hips into the air while straightening your arms and legs.

Holding this posture for a few minutes helps promote full body detoxification and stimulate the body's energy pathways. This posture can also strengthen digestion, reduce fatigue, and open up any blockages in the spine. Practicing this pose regularly can help improve one's overall health and well-being, making it an essential practice for those striving towards Ghata in their Kundalini awakening journey.

4. Salabasana

The practice of Salabasana for Ghata, or the cleansing stage of Kundalini awakening, has been used for centuries in yogic traditions. It is a powerful technique used to clear stagnant energy from the body and mind, which can arise from physical or mental health issues. To perform this exercise properly, one should move into the posture with deep breaths and stay there for at least five minutes. First, start by lying on your stomach and slowly lift your chest off the floor while arching your back. Doing this opens up any blockages that may be present in our energy pathways.

As the energy starts to flow freely, a feeling of light begins to spread through the body. An increased sense of inner peace follows this as blockages are cleared away. Mentally and emotionally, one can feel energized and uplifted due to the transformation in energy flow throughout the body. All of this culminates in a greater sense of self-awareness and deeper connection with one's inner divine potential that all yogis strive towards, making Salabasana for Ghata both a spiritually enriching and fulfilling experience.

5. Setubandhasana

By practicing Setubandhasana, you can unlock the dormant Kundalini energy within yourself and awaken its true potential. This asana, sometimes called *the bridge pose*, clears energetic blockages from the body and cultivates a heightened level of spirituality. To perform the pose properly, you must begin by sitting comfortably on the ground with your knees bent and your feet placed flat on either side of your hips. Ensure that your spine remains straight as you slowly begin to arch upward, gradually lifting your hips until your legs and torso make a "bridge" shape before returning to the starting position. As you practice this pose more often, you may notice a gradual increase in energy that brings with it improved clarity of thought and tranquility in lifestyle choices.

Pranayama Practices for Ghata

Ghata is about cleansing and purifying the energy field for us to be ready to take on the journey ahead. Pranayama resets our system, making it more receptive to the spiritual energy that awaits us. These practices range from breathwork to mantra chanting and visualization. Each practice has its energy associated with it, allowing us to connect with our inner power and open our chakras up for growth. Pranayama also increases our vital life force, which can, in turn, give us the strength to enhance and deepen our spiritual experiences. Despite being a critical aspect of Kundalini awakening, these practices are easy and beneficial for anyone who wants to reconnect with the divine within.

1. Nadi Shodhana

Nadi Shodhana Pranayama is an essential practice for the Ghata, or the cleansing stage, of the Kundalini awakening. This pranayama effectively cleanses the subtle energy channels and improves their health. Through this practice, we may experience intense feelings of joy, contentment, and peace that come from removing blockages in our energetic bodies. You can practice Nadi Shodhana Pranayama anywhere since no specific space or equipment is necessary.

Begin by sitting comfortably and then shifting your attention inward to focus on your breath. Allow your inhales and exhales to become long and slow as you move through this gentle practice. As you continue to practice the Nadi Shodhana Pranayama regularly, you will notice significant improvements in your mental and emotional well-being.

2. Anuloma Viloma

Anuloma Viloma Pranayama releases blockages and imbalances for the practitioner to take part in more advanced forms of meditation. During this practice, the individual inhales through one nostril and exhales through another in a continuous pattern. They hold their breath briefly before beginning a new cycle. Anuloma Viloma purifies the *nadis* (energy channels) and increases their permeability to allow higher levels of *prana* (energy) to flow freely throughout the body. It also aids in de-stressing, clarity of thought, and relaxation, making it a beneficial practice for everyone regardless of whether Kundalini awakening is desired or not.

3. Bhramari

Bhramari Pranayama is an ancient breathing technique used in Kundalini yoga to help the practitioner achieve Ghata, the cleansing stage of the Kundalini awakening. This unique and powerful tool clears out physical and mental debris and opens up prana (life force) pathways within the body, allowing energy to flow more freely. The practice involves inhaling deeply through the nose while simultaneously pressing on the tragus, a small protrusion on the earlobe. At the same time, a gentle humming sound is generated inwardly to energize and balance all seven chakras. Remember that practitioners must use self-regulation when practicing Bhramari Pranayama as it can become quite intense, so don't be afraid to take breaks or reduce intensities as needed.

Regardless of the stage of your Kundalini awakening, always end the practice with a sense of gratitude. Thank yourself for taking the time to reconnect with your spiritual self and be present at that moment. Bring awareness to any changes you may have noticed throughout the Ghata stage and take some time to integrate those into your life. This is an essential part of the process, allowing you to honor and appreciate your inner journey. Take a few deep breaths, open your eyes, and slowly return to your physical body. Finally, take some time to sit in silence and allow any lingering energetic shifts or feelings to settle completely within your being. Namaste!

Chapter 9: Pacihaya And Nishpatti: Unlocking Your Crown

Once you've moved through the first two stages of Kundalini awakening, you can move on to the next two stages of this journey, Pacihaya and Nishpatti. Pacihaya is the absorption stage where Kundalini energy moves throughout the whole body instead of just focusing on particular chakras. Nishpatti is the final stage of awakening and marks a massive shift in consciousness. This chapter will discuss the different kriyas and practices you can do to experience Pacihaya and Nishpatti. The Pacihaya and Nishpatti stages of Kundalini awakening are both crucial for reaching the highest states of spiritual consciousness. So, let's dive into what you need to know about these stages.

Pacihaya: The Absorption Stage

Pacihaya, otherwise known as the absorption stage of Kundalini awakening, is a significant part of spiritual development. During this stage, practitioners allow themselves to fully absorb and integrate newfound spiritual knowledge as they journey further along their chosen path. Access to Pacihaya can be through rituals, meditations, or even more intense techniques such as yoga or pranayama breathing exercises. One's ability to reach this state of understanding lies in trusting the power of universal energy to guide you and help you explore unfamiliar depths within yourself. When done correctly, this practice can bring about a transcendent sense of enlightenment, compassion for all living beings, unconditional love for oneself and others, and a connection with the divine realms.

A. What Happens during Pacihaya

Pacihaya, or the absorption stage of Kundalini awakening, describes the remarkable process when an individual becomes aware of their connection to their true self and ultimately to a higher form of divine power. During this phase of spiritual growth, individuals can experience anything from raising energy in their body's spine as emotion-filled energy to removing layers of inhibition and fear that were blocking pathways to joy.

Many in this phase often talk about inner tranquility and physical sensations that help them reach new heights of awareness. Along with profound feelings, strong visuals and higher mental clarity can accompany Pacihaya as the individual moves towards heightened spiritual understanding. In essence, the absorption stage is a beautiful moment in life where one can begin discovering more meaningful insight into the bigger picture around them, creating opportunities for expanded growth in a spiritual realm.

B. Chakras Affected and Their Effects

The energy of a Kundalini awakening is intense and can cause an intoxicating array of sensations. Pacihaya involves the mind drawing energy from various chakras as it progresses. The lower chakras will draw in physical energies such as passion and divine love, whereas the upper chakras absorb emotional energies like clarity and joy. During this process, there may be feelings of trembling and surging, as well as psychosomatic disturbances. Through this process, however, people reach a heightened state of consciousness, allowing them to tap into profound levels of awareness not experienced during the normal flow of everyday life.

C. How Pacihaya Is Different from Other Stages

How the energy of Pacihaya is experienced is different from that of other Kundalini awakening stages as it does not move from one main chakra to another as the other stages do. Rather, it spreads throughout the entire body from its point of origin in the heart chakra. This is why it is known as the absorption stage – since its purpose is to allow practitioners to absorb and integrate newfound spiritual knowledge instead of just traveling from one chakra to the next.

Kundalini Kriyas to Trigger Pacihaya

Kundalini kriyas are powerful, breath-based exercises designed to help activate and open our energy channels so that Kundalini energy can be released and expand throughout the body. These kriyas, when performed correctly, will enable us to reach the Pacihaya state during a Kundalini awakening. Pacihaya is an energized resting stage where we absorb the potent vibrations from the awakened energy and integrate them with our spiritual awareness.

To achieve this calming yet liberating feeling, it's crucial to incorporate breathing exercises, visualization techniques like focusing on a healing color such as blue or purple, gentle movements like swaying back and forth or spinning around in circles, and mantra chanting that clears out negative mental energies. When practiced consistently, these kriyas will lead you on a journey to deeper levels of connection with your inner self, one in which you feel enlightened and ready for whatever comes next.

1. Sat Kriya

Sat Kriya is an ancient technique that works in the energetic realm to connect a person's physical and spiritual bodies. Performing Sat Kriya has been hailed as possibly the most effective tool for initiating Pacihaya, the absorption stage of Kundalini awakening. This mystical practice opens up one's energy systems, enabling a more powerful and integrated connection with our inner wisdom and divine nature.

The practice involves channeling pranic (life force) energy up and down the spine, affecting both the physical and subtle bodies while producing peaceful mental states that lead to profound inner transformation. Sat Kriya, along with other techniques, can be helpful during Pacihaya, thus allowing individuals to imbibe divine energy into their bodies to experience greater gains in awareness and meaningful shifts in consciousness.

2. Om Chanting

Om chanting is increasingly being used to trigger the absorption stage of Kundalini awakening. By focusing your energy on the sound of Om and repeating it as you meditate, you can awaken the dormant source of Kundalini's power within you. Generally, if this stage is successful, those who have done it can experience an infusion of spiritual energy throughout their body and mind. Beyond leading to higher levels of consciousness, this heightened awareness can open pathways for creative insight and profound understanding. Om chanting is a powerful tool for unlocking our inner potential and helps us move one step closer to enlightenment.

3. Surrender and Breathwork

Breathwork and surrender are two seemingly opposite approaches to experiencing the absorption stage of Kundalini awakening. To experience Pacihaya, both must be part of your practice, allowing yourself to breathe deeply with awareness and consciously giving up control. With each deep breath, we cultivate a deeper level of relaxation in our body and mind. As we increasingly relax into our natural state of surrender, we start recognizing the inner power that brings greater clarity in both thought and emotion through the acceptance and appreciation of all life has to offer. When we can make these conscious connections, our Pacihaya journey begins as we move toward understanding our true potential as spiritual beings in an energy-filled world.

4. Khechari Mudra

Khechari Mudra, a powerful practice for activating the inner spiritual potential in yoga, is said to be pivotal in triggering Pacihaya, the absorption stage of the Kundalini awakening. This mudra involves pressing your tongue upward toward the soft palate while gently double-rolling it backward and sealing it against the uvula. This complex process unleashes energy that can be directed via awareness toward any chakra. When done regularly, perception and understanding of deep, underlying energy fields truly amplify. In addition to physical benefits such as improved digestion and better overall health, this mudra brings clarity to all areas of life, providing a sense of balance that empowers one with greater mental capacity and focus.

5. Bandhas

To get to the Pacihaya stage, one must train their body and mind to push through blockages so that vital energy can flow freely. One way to do this is by using bandhas exercises. Bandhas involve contracting certain muscles which redirect prana, or life force energy. Try holding the *mula bandha*, or root lock, engaging your pelvic floor muscles and pulling them up. Similarly, to practice *nauli*, you need to first contract your abdominal muscles and then isolate certain sections of the abdomen by further contracting certain regions with a circular motion. This activates the solar plexus chakra, which is connected to our Kundalini energy. Once practiced regularly, bandhas unblock energy pathways that are inhibiting our spiritual growth and allow us to progress further into the Pacihaya stage.

Nishpatti: The Final Stage

Nishpatti is the final stage of elevating consciousness and tapping into the immense power that lies deep within. This ultimately leads to a deeper insight into truths and an intensified connection with one's inner being. During this process, various mental, emotional, and physical breakdowns are experienced as higher states of awareness are met. It marks an enlightening step in life as the awakened Kundalini energy brings about self-realization and liberation from the mundane cycles of life. It is an undeniably powerful experience for those brave enough to embark on this journey of self-discovery as they ultimately unlock their spiritual potential.

A. What to Expect during Nishpatti

In the final stage of Kundalini's awakening, you'll no longer be guided by any force outside of itself and instead gain an absolute connection with your energy. As the energy ascends, you'll feel a heightened sense of self-awareness and a deep understanding of the world surrounding you. Furthermore, this state of being can bring immense joy and contentment as you come to understand yourself on a more meaningful level. During Nishpatti, stay open to whatever unfolds in the inner journey and use healing practices such as meditation to further enhance the connection with your true self.

B. Consciousness Expansion

Consciousness expansion during Nishpatti, the final stage of the Kundalini awakening, is an incredibly special experience. It is often called a state of enlightenment and oneness with the universe. During this period, one's awareness of oneself and the world around you is much more expanded. This greater sense of understanding can help you connect more meaningfully with other people and become more attuned to their internal needs. It also gives practitioners a better appreciation for the beauty in our world, helping us see life from a higher perspective. Ultimately, the state of consciousness expansion that comes during Nishpatti can offer an incredible sense of balance, peace, and insight into our true inner selves.

Kundalini Kriyas to Trigger Nishpatti

In Kundalini yoga, kriyas are used to trigger the final stage of the Kundalini awakening. This process involves spiritual self-realization and promises peace of mind and body to attain a higher consciousness. A variety of kriyas can be used during this process, from meditation, chanting mantras, and spiritual breathing exercises. To reach the highest level is to stay disciplined with your practice by being consistent and focused. The journey is different for each individual, as every person has their own way of working through struggles and achieving liberation. All these factors come together through practicing Kundalini kriyas so that the ultimate goal, triggering Nishpatti, can finally be attained.

1. Pranayama

Pranayama is an indispensable tool for those seeking to awaken their Kundalini energy. It is said that by mastering this yogic practice, we can come one step closer to reaching the final stage of Kundalini awakening. Pranayama consists of rhythmic and continual breath control whereby we can send fresh oxygen and vital energy throughout our body and clear any blockages hindering the ascension of our Kundalini. This type of breath work also promotes balance within our body and mind, further assisting in the activation of Kundalini. Thus, with sufficient practice and dedication, we can reach Nishpatti's sublime state through Pranayama, where true liberation awaits us.

2. Mantra Meditation

Mantra meditation is one of the most effective methods for triggering Kundalini awakening. By focusing intently on a powerful and meaningful mantra or sound, a person can tap into their higher inner potential and eventually experience the ultimate stage of spiritual transformation. This process works best when done in an atmosphere of peace, stillness, and awareness. It also requires perseverance, dedication, and total devotion to reach a "state of consciousness beyond all duality." Ultimately, this type of spiritual practice connects individuals to their inner divinity, enabling them to attain true enlightenment.

3. Visualization and Affirmations

Learning how to trigger Nishpatti through visualization and affirmations is a powerful way to become more attuned to your spiritual growth. Visualization is a type of meditation that can guide us in accessing our inner realms, while affirmations are conscious statements of the truth we want to embody and the purpose we have chosen for ourselves from within our deepest being. When used together, visualizations and affirmations can empower us to realize our mind-body-soul and tap into deeper levels of consciousness for greatness. Visualization directs our energy toward what we desire most, while affirmations provide repeated confirmation that reinforces the power of this sacred process. With practice, anyone can learn techniques for visualization and affirmations to trigger Nishpatti, ultimately helping their manifest destiny come alive.

4. Kundalini Yoga Postures

Kundalini positions are an effective way to open the blocks that stand in the way of Kundalini awakening. When used with skill, they can be effective tools to help the practitioner reach Nishpatti. Through practice, one can use these postures to clear energy blockages, activate physical, emotional, and mental healing, and restore vitality and clarity to one's life. Examples of postures beneficial for triggering Nishpatti are deep abdominal breathing, spinal twists, shoulder stands, cat-cow stretches, Vajrasana or "thunderbolt squat" posture, meditation practices such as mantra chanting, and more. Each posture has its purpose and impact on achieving higher self-awareness. You can move into a full spiritual awakening with practice, patience, and perseverance.

5. Pratyahara

Pratyahara, the act of internal concentration and withdrawal from external engagement or activities, is an essential step to trigger Nishpatti. This practice develops greater powers of focus, which lead to a heightened state of spiritual awareness and helps to raise dormant energies through the body. Through regular practice of Pratyahara, one tunes into their inner energy and can then elevate that energy to higher levels. Furthermore, by engaging in this level of self-discovery, practitioners experience insights into their own spiritual identity and come closer to mastering inner peace. Pratyahara sets you up for Kundalini awakening and allows you to experience inner realms of pure bliss and divine realization during your journey.

Kundalini awakening is a powerful phenomenon that requires dedication and patience, but with the right techniques and practices, such as visualization and affirmations, postures, and Pratyahara, you can reach the ultimate stage of the Kundalini awakening. Regular practice allows one to become more connected to their inner being and mobilize energies within the body to better understand the divine and the self. With this newfound awareness, you can experience a profound transformation and move closer to fully awakening your Kundalini energy.

Chapter 10: Kundalini Energy Is Awakened, Now What?

Kundalini awakening can be an intense and sometimes overwhelming experience, as it is a process of spiritual growth involving major shifts in consciousness. By understanding the process and having access to the right resources and guidance, you can accept and lead a happy life with your expanded consciousness. Experiencing a Kundalini awakening can be life-changing, but it doesn't always come without consequences. When an individual's Kundalini energy is awakened to the point where it is overactive, it can cause physical and emotional discomfort, making it difficult for them to adjust to and cope with the effects.

Often intertwined with intense spiritual experience, overactive Kundalini can be overwhelming and stress the body and mind too much. In this chapter, we will advise how to accept your new consciousness and offer Kundalini yoga kriyas, techniques, and sequences to tame an overactive Kundalini. Finally, we will discuss calming techniques to help you adjust if your Kundalini awakening was unintentional. This chapter aims to help you gain confidence in managing your Kundalini energy and living a fulfilling life with it.

Accept Your New Consciousness

The awakening of your Kundalini energy is a special and powerful experience. It can be difficult to let go of the beliefs and mental patterns you have accustomed to, but it is worth it. Once your Kundalini energy is awakened, you have been given a chance to grow into something new, something beautiful and expanded in consciousness. Accepting your new self is key to fully utilizing the potential that this life-changing transformation has unlocked within you. Allow yourself to explore and find comfort in any shifts, recognitions, or personal discoveries you may encounter on this journey of self-discovery.

Kundalini Yoga Kriyas to Tame an Overactive Kundalini

An overactive Kundalini is an alarming condition for many who seek spiritual development. Without proper guidance and understanding of the energy's reactiveness, it can have devastating effects on your emotional, physical, and psychological health. The entirety of the individual will be subjected to the intense vibrations generated by an overactive Kundalini that can cause a range of physiological symptoms, from anxiety and sleeplessness to lack of clarity in thoughts and hyperactivity. The flow of uncontrolled energy can easily put too much strain on the body, making it turbulent. Here are some Kundalini yoga kriyas and techniques which you can use to tame an overactive Kundalini.

1. Heart Chakra Meditation

In times of chaos, it can be difficult to find peace. One way to do so is through heart chakra meditation. This practice calms and balances the Kundalini energy at the spine's base. By grounding yourself in the present moment with deep breathing exercises and visualizations, you can inspire a sense of peacefulness throughout your mind and body while harnessing your life force energy. Heart chakra meditation also brings intention into each movement and helps us to cultivate self-love as we accept our current circumstances.

To begin, sit comfortably with your spine erect and your legs crossed. Close your eyes and bring awareness to the heart chakra located at the center of your chest. Visualize a white light radiating from the center of your chest and extending outwards in all directions. Focus on the breath as you inhale and exhale deeply, allowing your body to relax more with every inhalation and exhalation. With continued practice, we can begin to overcome everyday struggles and create harmony within ourselves and our environment.

2. Breath Awareness

There are many complex pathways to self-awareness, but breath awareness is always essential for unlocking dormant energies like the Kundalini. By using slow, deep breaths and focusing on the sensation of air flowing through the body, you'll enter a meditative state that may soothe and excite your innermost consciousness. While this alone does not result in the awakening of Kundalini, it serves as a platform for one's spirit to travel and seek peace within you. This process requires patience, love, and discipline but can bring forth greatness in terms of spiritual growth and understanding of inner power. So let go with breath awareness, reach out with your awareness, and access an enlightened way of living.

3. Mantra Japa

Mantra Japa is a centuries-old, powerful spiritual practice that tames an overactive Kundalini. In this practice, the individual chants sacred mantras and syllables out loud or in their minds, repeating them with intention and focus. Through this practice, deeper layers of their unconscious are accessed and energized. It works to bring balance by activating the chakras, which can ground and center an overexcited Kundalini. Anyone looking to find stillness in their Kundalini energy should try Mantra Japa. Its calming effect can be felt almost immediately, leading to an overall sense of peace, happiness, and well-being.

4. Asanas and Mudras

A range of yoga poses and mudras can tame an overactive Kundalini. These involve carefully placing the body into specific poses and mudras, which activate the subtle energies of the body. Asanas and mudras focus on particular energetic points to direct the flow of energy, aiding in releasing any blockages or constraints that may be keeping the Kundalini from achieving balance. Here are some poses which can be used for this purpose:

- **Gomukhasana (Cow Face Pose):** This pose calms the mind and body by releasing tension from the shoulders and neck. It also helps stimulate the central nervous system and the endocrine glands.
- **Baddha Konasana (Butterfly Pose):** This pose stretches the inner thighs and opens up the hip area. It also brings an overall sense of relaxation to the body.
- **Matsyasana (Fish Pose):** This pose strengthens the spine and opens up the chest area. It also reduces fatigue and stress by

calming the mind.

- **Ardha Matsyendrasana (Half Lord of the Fishes Pose):** This pose reduces stress and fatigue by stimulating the spine, hips, abdomen, and chest area.
- **Padmasana (Lotus Pose):** This pose calms the mind and body by releasing tension from the hips and legs. It also helps to stimulate the central nervous system.
- **Pran Mudra:** This mudra balances the energy flow in the body and brings a sense of focus and clarity.

Sequences to Tame an Overactive Kundalini

Uncontrolled activation of Kundalini can hurt the body and mind. To regulate it, special sequences of breath work and postures have been created to help tame an overactive Kundalini. These sequences are designed to awaken clear energy paths in the body and balance out energy levels, restoring balance and harmony in both body and soul. With regular practice, these sequences can bring tangible results and help open the door to deeper states of consciousness.

1. Balancing Sequence

Balancing the flow of Kundalini energy throughout the body is critical for mental and physical health. The correct sequence of yoga poses can help achieve this balance without injury or strain. Forward bends are a calming yoga pose that can strengthen muscles, relax the mind, and bring awareness to the spine. Backbends engage and strengthen the heart center, reversing any blockages in energetic pathways, followed by twists that flush out any toxins and create more flexibility in the spine. Finally, inversions provide many benefits, like reducing stress levels and boosting alertness. Regularly following this sequence of forward bends, backbends, twists, and inversions can maintain the natural flow of Kundalini energy throughout your body.

2. Kundalini Awakening Sequence

This sequence is designed to awaken the Kundalini and create a deep connection between body and soul. To start, Nadi Shodhan Pranayama, a traditional breathing technique, can be used to balance the nervous system and awaken the chakras. It is followed by Surya Namaskar, or Sun Salutations, which helps build heat in the body and create an energy flow from head to toe. The next step is to do a series of asanas and mudras to open up the blocked energy points in the body, allowing Kundalini to rise. Finally, meditation can calm the mind and allow for an effortless connection with divine wisdom.

3. Chakra Cleansing Sequence

The chakras are energy centers that need to be balanced and cleansed regularly. This sequence is designed to open, clear, and balance the chakras throughout the body. Grounding poses like Tadasana (Mountain Pose) can be used to connect with the Earth's energy. Ujjayi Pranayama can be used to bring awareness and clarity to the mind. Next, a series of asanas can be used to activate each chakra. Finally, meditation can cleanse the chakras and create space for inner stillness.

4. Prana Vayu Balancing Sequence

Prana Vayu is the life force energy that flows through the body and helps maintain health. This sequence is designed to open up a stuck Prana, promote a healthy flow of life force energy throughout the body and bring balance and harmony. To start, Nadi Shodhan Pranayama can create an even flow of energy throughout the body. A series of standing, seated, and inverted poses can open up all the energy centers in the body. Finally, meditation can be used to unite with Universal energies and promote a lasting sense of well-being.

By practicing these sequences regularly, you'll experience a deeper connection between your physical and energetic bodies allowing for a healthier, happier life. Remember to always take your time when practicing and listen to what your body is telling you, as it will guide you toward the best path for self-discovery.

Calming an Unintended Kundalini Awakening

Kundalini awakening can be both an exciting and a terrifying experience. The energy unlocked through this phenomenon can be very strong and even lead to trance-like states of consciousness if left unchecked. However, while some people seek out Kundalini awakenings intentionally, there are many whose awakenings happen unintentionally and can be difficult to manage.

Fortunately, yoga practitioners have developed techniques to calm an unintended Kundalini awakening, such as focusing on breathwork or visualizing the energy connecting different chakras in your body. Meditation is also helpful in lowering stress levels and allowing the energetic waves to safely ease out of one's body. Other activities, such as yoga poses and physical or creative outlets, may be beneficial when managing an unintended Kundalini awakening.

A. Preparing the Body and Mind

When Kundalini energy is awakened, it can cause increased physical and mental arousal, which can be quite uncomfortable. Relaxation techniques such as yoga, breathwork, and meditation are recommended to prepare the body and mind for a calm and peaceful state. This allows us to clear energetic blockages from our energy centers in the body which supports the information needed for calming an unintended Kundalini awakening. Mindfulness can also play a crucial role in preparation as it brings awareness to our thoughts and feelings accompanying the process. By implementing steps that address physiological and psychological needs, we can create a safe space necessary for achieving a well-balanced state of inner peace.

B. Grounding Techniques

To quell the intensity of a Kundalini experience, grounding techniques are beneficial in calming the process. These techniques involve focusing on the senses, such as feeling the contact of one's feet on solid ground or hands saturating in cold water. One could also focus on something outside themselves, such as a tree with its roots firmly planted in the earth. All of these techniques bring attention back to the body and away from any other mental distractions that might arise during an unintended awakening. Using grounding techniques will bring a sense of safety and a level of control that aids in successfully navigating bouts of intense energy.

C. Releasing Stored Negative Energy

Releasing stored negative energy is essential to calming an unintended Kundalini awakening. Kundalini is healing energy within all of us, but if it is released too quickly or without proper guidance, it can bring up issues that we never even knew were there. That's why releasing stored negative energy properly is so critical. Breathing, yoga, and meditation are just a few ways to accomplish this.

Taking the time to be mindful and connect with yourself on a deeper level can help you rid yourself of any underlying blocks or tension held within your body and spirit. Kundalini knows no bounds, but with respect and dedication, it can create positive results in our lives. Moving through the process of releasing stored negative energy with self-love and compassion can bring rhythm and balance back into our lives and make our relationship with Kundalini more powerful than ever before.

D. Connecting with Nature

Being in nature is a powerful and calming method to address an unintended Kundalini awakening. It reminds us of the interconnectedness of all life and our surroundings and gives us a sense of connection to something greater than ourselves. The beauty of nature can provide insight into oneself, bringing clarity to the inner turmoil created by the Kundalini process. Taking slow, mindful walks in nature allows us to be present in each moment, from the shape of leaves to the sound of birds singing or the feeling of soil beneath our feet. Being conscious of our senses allows us to look inward for understanding as we navigate this unexpected journey of physical, emotional, and spiritual transformation.

E. Connecting with Others

Connecting with others when trying to calm an unintended Kundalini awakening can also work well. Working closely with a spiritual advisor, healer, or coach can help you focus your energy on ways to cope and create inner balance. Sharing insights and stories, such as dreams and symbols related to Kundalini energy patterns, is also a great way to gain clarity amid an experience that may sometimes feel chaotic and overwhelming. This can help you develop insight into the root causes of the awakening to more fully appreciate and understand it. Moreover, talking and listening with other people who have gone through similar experiences can be empowering. Ultimately, connecting with others who are familiar with Kundalini energy allows us to share a feeling of solidarity as we journey through this transformative process.

The journey of Kundalini awakening can be intense and chaotic, but with the right tools and practices, we can learn to navigate it more gracefully. By grounding ourselves, releasing stored negative energy, connecting with nature, and connecting with others who understand the process, we can find a sense of clarity within the storm. This process ultimately allows us to discover our core power and potential, creating a harmonious relationship with this mysterious energy. Accepting and embracing the journey of Kundalini awakening is an act of courage that can lead to a profound transformation in our lives.

Glossary of Terms

Several Hindu terms and concepts related to Kundalini have been used throughout this book. For reference, here is an alphabetized list of these terms and their meanings or English translations.

Agni: Fire, used to describe the Kundalini force rising through the chakras

Ajna: Also known as the third eye, it is located between the eyebrows and is considered a major energy center.

Anahata: Another major energy center situated in the chest and associated with the heart.

Arambha: The first stage of awakening the Kundalini energy

Ardha Matsyendrasana: Half Lord of the Fishes Pose, a yoga posture used to stimulate the Kundalini

Asana: Yoga posture

Chakra: The circular energy centers along the spine of a practitioner, each with its color and purpose

Drishti: A focused gaze used in certain yoga postures

Ghata: The cleansing stage of Kundalini awakening, followed right after Arambha.

Kriya: A series of yoga poses, breathing exercises, and meditation practices used to activate the Kundalini

Kundalini: The spiritual energy located at the base of the spine that can be activated through yoga and meditation

Mantra: A sacred sound or phrase used for meditation and spiritual development

Manipura: The third chakra, located in the navel area and associated with confidence and self-esteem

Mudra: A symbolic hand gesture used in yoga and meditation

Muladhara: The root chakra at the base of the spine

Nadi: An energy channel

Nishpatti: The final stage of awakening Kundalini, in which the practitioner feels a state of oneness and inner peace

Pacihaya: The absorption stage of Kundalini awakening, the stage after Ghata

Prana: The life force that sustains the body

Pranayama: The practice of controlling and regulating the breath

Saraswati: Goddess of knowledge and creativity, often associated with the Kundalini

Shakti: The feminine divine energy often associated with the Kundalini

Svadhishthana: The second chakra, located at the lower abdomen area and associated with emotions

Uddiyana Bandha: Abdominal lock used to draw the Kundalini energy up through the spine.

Vishuddha: The fifth chakra, located at the throat and associated with communication.

Yoga: A set of physical, mental, and spiritual practices used to awaken the Kundalini.

Yoni Mudra: A hand gesture used to help focus the mind, often associated with the practice of awakening the Kundalini.

Yogi: One who practices yoga, meditation, and other spiritual disciplines to cultivate the Kundalini energy.

Conclusion

The ancient, awe-inspiring journey of Kundalini Shakti has been a transformative practice for centuries, connecting individuals to their innermost selves. Every experience is unique, as each person undergoes a different internal transformation. In this process, an awakening of energy is initiated throughout the body. This state brings about profound states of deep meditation and heightened sensory awareness, allowing for great insight into the inner workings of oneself.

The journey can be accompanied by a range of emotions, gradually moving towards greater understanding and acceptance of one's spiritual center. Powerful transformations such as these remind each individual to reach deep within and discover a greater purpose connected with their soul.

Identity is an ever-evolving process that changes as we grow and experience life. As one develops a stronger understanding of themselves, expectations from the outside world seem much less significant. This can be difficult but immensely rewarding as we learn more about our own needs and desires. We become more in tune with what brings us the most fulfillment, accepting our whole self so that we may become present in life with a newfound sense of understanding and empowerment.

Kundalini Shakti is a dynamic energy source that is an energetic guide for individuals seeking self-awareness and personal growth. It is often found within the depths of the unconscious mind, prompting bold exploration that can lead to a discovery of one's true identity and purpose. Those with an open mindset willing to listen to their inner voice and explore the unseen realms within can make great strides towards understanding themselves and their paths. Kundalini Shakti encourages deep contemplation and introspection, offering insight into energy centers hidden away in the depths of the soul that can help one decipher even the most mysterious paths in life.

This guide served as an introduction to Kundalini Shakti and its potential for promoting personal growth and enlightenment. The preceding chapters have discussed the importance of understanding one's chakras, preparing for Kundalini meditation, and learning the essential tools to unlock the energy within. The benefits of awakening this powerful energy and how it can help us on our journey to understanding ourselves have been explored. The four stages of Kundalini energy, Arambha, Ghata, Pacihaya, and Nishpatti, were each explored in depth.

Ultimately, we were reminded that each of us has the potential to tap into the power within, and Kundalini Shakti can serve as a reliable source for unlocking our greatest potential. With a deeper understanding of self and a greater awareness of our spiritual realm, we can begin to take the first steps toward unlocking true power and potential within ourselves. Welcome to the journey of Kundalini Shakti! May it be full of joy and revelations.

Here's another book by Mari Silva that you might like

Your Free Gift
(only available for a limited time)

Thanks for getting this book! If you want to learn more about various spirituality topics, then join Mari Silva's community and get a free guided meditation MP3 for awakening your third eye. This guided meditation mp3 is designed to open and strengthen ones third eye so you can experience a higher state of consciousness. Simply visit the link below the image to get started.

https://spiritualityspot.com/meditation

<u>Or, Scan the QR code!</u>

References

The College of Psychic Studies : Enlighten : What is a psychic attack. (n.d.). The College of Psychic Studies. https://www.collegeofpsychicstudies.co.uk/enlighten/what-is-a-psychic-attack/

Leigh, J. (2018, May 31). Psychic Protection. Spirituality & Health. https://www.spiritualityhealth.com/articles/2018/05/31/psychic-protection

Mara. (2011, July 22). Boundaries and Psychic Protection. WholeSpirit → Shamanic Counselor ∴ Intuitive Consultant ∴ Energy Healer ∴ Personal Evolution Through Nature-Based Shamanic Healing & Shamanic Training. https://www.wholespirit.com/boundaries-and-psychic-protection/

Boundaries and psychic protection ∴ WholeSpirit. (2011, July 22). WholeSpirit → Shamanic Counselor ∴ Intuitive Consultant ∴ Energy Healer ∴ Personal Evolution Through Nature-Based Shamanic Healing & Shamanic Training; Whole Spirit LLC. https://www.wholespirit.com/boundaries-and-psychic-protection/

Earthmonk. (2022, January 7). 8 powerful ways to protect your spiritual energy. Earthmonk. https://earthmonk.guru/8-powerful-ways-to-protect-spiritual-energy/

Insight Network, Inc. (n.d.). Insight timer - #1 free meditation app for sleep, relax & more. Insighttimer.com. https://insighttimer.com/stevenobel/guided-meditations/psychic-protection-meditation

Leigh, J. (2018, May 31). Psychic protection. Spirituality & Health. https://www.spiritualityhealth.com/articles/2018/05/31/psychic-protection

Stardust, L. (2019, May 28). How to use magic to banish energy vampires. Teen Vogue. https://www.teenvogue.com/story/how-to-use-magic-to-banish-energy-vampires

Why protection is important in healing and psychic work. (2022, March 10). Giancarlo Serra. https://www.giancarloserra.org/why-protection-is-important-in-healing-and-psychic-work/

Zukav, G. (2015, April 1). How to protect your spiritual energy. Oprah.com. https://www.oprah.com/inspiration/protecting-your-spiritual-energy

Cass. (2022, August 7). 5 meditations to raise your vibration. Manifesting Harmony. https://manifestingharmony.com/tools/meditations-to-raise-your-vibration/

Coughlin, S. (2015, October 21). 5 medium-approved tips to develop your own psychic powers. Refinery29.com; Refinery29. https://www.refinery29.com/en-us/how-to-improve-intuition

Cronkleton, E. (2018, May 15). What is aromatherapy and how does it help me? Healthline. https://www.healthline.com/health/what-is-aromatherapy

Estrada, J. (2019, September 11). What it actually means to raise your vibrational energy—plus 12 ways to do it. Well+Good. https://www.wellandgood.com/vibrational-energy/

How to raise your vibration instantly? (2021, May 21). Times of India Blog. https://timesofindia.indiatimes.com/readersblog/theenchantedpen/how-to-raise-your-vibration-instantly-32251/

Irven, J. (2020, March 29). 19 ways to raise your vibration — sustainable bliss. Sustainable Bliss | Self-Care and Intentional Living. https://www.sustainableblissco.com/journal/raising-your-vibration

Jones, E. (2009). Aromatherapy. In Massage for Therapists (pp. 163–178). Wiley-Blackwell.

Mahakatha, A. (2023, January 16). Best guided meditation to raise vibration. Mahakatha Blog. https://mahakatha.com/blog/best-guided-meditation-to-raise-vibration

McGinley, K. (2019, September 18). How to raise your emotional & spiritual vibration. Chopra. https://chopra.com/articles/a-complete-guide-to-raise-your-vibration

Raypole, C. (2021, May 5). Metta meditation for mother's day.

Rebecca Joy Stanborough, M. F. A. (2020, November 13). What is vibrational energy? Healthline. https://www.healthline.com/health/vibrational-energy

Rose, S. (2022, February 28). 15 ways to raise your vibrations. Sahara Rose. https://iamsahararose.com/blog/a-guide-on-how-to-raise-your-vibrations/

Sara. (2021, April 10). 35 affirmations to raise your vibration instantly. Spiritvibez. https://spiritvibez.com/35-affirmations-to-raise-your-vibration/

Top 4 breathing practices to raise your vibration. (2020, May 20). YogaVibes. https://www.yogavibes.com/blog/meditation-pranayama/raise-vibration-breathing-practice/

What is reiki, and does it really work? (2021, August 30). Cleveland Clinic. https://health.clevelandclinic.org/reiki/

Basic Buddhist teachings - III. (2021, April 14). Theravada. https://www.theravada.gr/en/about-buddhism/understanding-karma/

Darren. (2012, March 7). The 4 dimensions of energy: Physical, emotional, mental and spiritual. UpStartist. https://upstartist.tv/mba/the-4-dimensions-of-energy/

Stuck feeling stagnant? 14 spiritual cleansing methods to clear it out. (2023, February 24). Mindbodygreen. https://www.mindbodygreen.com/articles/spiritual-cleansing

Thomas, P. (2019, October 9). Your 4 types of energy. Self Help for Life. https://selfhelpforlife.com/master-your-energy/

(N.d.-a). Yogabasics.comhttps://www.yogabasics.com/connect/yoga-blog/spiritual-cleansing/

(N.d.-b). Goop.comhttps://goop.com/wellness/spirituality/the-four-bodies/

6 ways to purify your space – KonMari. (2019, November 12). KonMari | The Official Website of Marie Kondo; KonMari Media, Inc. https://konmari.com/home-purification/

10 easy ways to cleanse your home of negative energy. (2012, April 3). Mindbodygreen. https://www.mindbodygreen.com/articles/how-to-cleanse-your-home-of-negative-energy

Bunch, E. (2019, April 3). 4 ways to set the right intention for your home with a cleansing prayer. Well+Good. https://www.wellandgood.com/prayer-to-say-when-saging-your-house/

Davis, F. (2022, April 11). Spiritual pet protection: Shield your dog or cat in positive energy. Karma and Luck. https://www.karmaandluck.com/blogs/news/spiritual-pet-protection

Helena. (2021, January 24). How to build an altar at home for spiritual self-care. Disorient.

How to clear negative energy around baby or older children. (n.d.). Go with Harmony. https://www.gowithharmony.com/clear-negative-energy-around-baby.html

Jay, S. (2022, August 3). 6 cleansing rituals for you & your home. Revoloon. https://revoloon.com/shanijay/cleansing-ritual

Oaks, M. (2020, September 29). House cleansing: A checklist for clearing bad energy from your home. Redfin | Real Estate Tips for Home Buying, Selling & More; Redfin. https://www.redfin.com/blog/clearing-bad-energy-from-your-home/

PURNAMA. (2020, July 15). Jak okadzać dom by pozbyć się negatywnej energii? PURNAMA.

Sanna. (2021, April 27). How to Cleanse the Energy in your Space using Incense. SANNA Conscious Concept. https://sannaconsciousconcept.com/how-to-cleanse-the-energy-in-your-space-using-incense

Stewart, T. (2021, October 17). Step by step: How to cleanse A space (energetically & spiritually). Whimsy Soul. https://whimsysoul.com/how-to-cleanse-a-space-energetically-and-spiritually/

The importance of purifying and cleansing your space before a big move. (2021, February 23).

Tiny carbons cure to clear negative energy you absorbed from other people. (n.d.). Go with Harmony. https://www.gowithharmony.com/cure-to-clear-negative-energy.html

Tuttle, C. (2020, October 19). 2 techniques to protect your child from negative energy. Carol Tuttle. https://ct.liveyourtruth.com/2-techniques-to-protect-your-child-from-negative-energy/

Why energy cleansing is important (and how to do it). (n.d.). AUTHOR KAREN FRAZIER. https://www.authorkarenfrazier.com/blog/why-energy-cleansing-is-important-and-how-to-do-it#/

(N.d.). Yogabasics.com. https://www.yogabasics.com/connect/yoga-blog/clear-negative-energy/

7 ways to reset your energy & cleanse your aura when you feel blocked. (2022, September 21). Mindbodygreen. https://www.mindbodygreen.com/articles/aura-cleansing

Marley, C. (2018, November 25). How to cleanse aura. Mental Health Resources & Articles | Plumm; Plummhealth. https://blog.plummhealth.com/fundamental-concepts/8-ways-to-cleanse-your-aura-from-negativity/

Tanaaz. (2016, April 26). The 7 layers of your aura. Forever Conscious. https://foreverconscious.com/7-layers-aura

Who stole my energy? How difficult people affect your aura. (2012, July 26). Mindbodygreen. https://www.mindbodygreen.com/articles/how-difficult-people-affect-your-aura-energy

(N.d.). Goop.com. https://goop.com/wellness/spirituality/healing-your-aura/

Bernstein, G. (2019, December 22). A Spirit Junkie Introduction to Archangels and Guardian Angels. Gabby Bernstein. https://gabbybernstein.com/angels/

pakosloski. (2022, April 6). Guardian Angel prayer for spiritual protection. Aleteia — Catholic Spirituality, Lifestyle, World News, and Culture. https://aleteia.org/2022/04/06/guardian-angel-prayer-for-spiritual-protection/

Insight Network, Inc. (n.d.). Psychic Protection With Archangel Michael. Insighttimer.Com. https://insighttimer.com/sarahhall444/guided-meditations/psychic-protection-with-archangel-michael

Richardson, T. C. (2021, May 25). How To Get To Know Your Guardian Angels + Unlock Their Power. Mindbodygreen. https://www.mindbodygreen.com/articles/how-to-get-to-know-your-guardian-angels

Megan, M. (2020, October 5). Divine Angel Summoning Sigils - Magick Megan. Medium. https://medium.com/@matohinle17/divine-angel-summoning-sigils-b75c2d70b620

eskarda. (2021, August 18). 5 Crystals for Protection From Negative Energy. Yoga Journal. https://www.yogajournal.com/lifestyle/crystals-for-protection/

Skon, J. (2023, January 13). 6 Crystals To Protect Yourself From Toxic People & Negative Energy. Mindbodygreen. https://www.mindbodygreen.com/articles/crystals-for-protection

Top 15 Spiritual Plants. (2020, December 24). Floweraura Blog. https://www.floweraura.com/blog/plants-care-n-tips/top-10-spiritual-plants

Growing, B. (2021, August 31). How To Use Houseplants for Spiritual Protection (14 Plants). Bean Growing. https://www.beangrowing.com/houseplants-for-spiritual-protection/

Vierck, J. (2022, March 23). Top 8 Powerful Protection Symbols & How to Use Them. Karma and Luck. https://www.karmaandluck.com/blogs/news/8-powerful-protection-symbols-how-to-use-them

Wang, C. (2022, May 10). 7 Spiritual Protection Symbols and Their Meanings. Buddha & Karma. https://buddhaandkarma.com/blogs/guide/spiritual-protection-symbols-meaning

Jennifer McVey, C. (2022, June 14). How to Make Sigils. WikiHow. https://www.wikihow.com/Make-Sigils

Kallima Spiritual Centre - Newsletter - July/August 2020. (n.d.). Flipbuilder.Com. https://online.flipbuilder.com/yjll/isvd/files/basic-html/page15.html

Wood, T. (2021, October 21). 10 Signs of Spiritual Attack. Evergreen Church. https://evcsj.org/2021-10-21-10-signs-of-spiritual-attack/

6 Easy Ways To Break A Magic Curse Or Hex. (2022, March 5). Eclectic Witchcraft. https://eclecticwitchcraft.com/break-a-magic-curse-or-hex/

Rose, M. (2022, December 8). StyleCaster. StyleCaster. https://stylecaster.com/how-to-use-protection-magic/

Alex. (2021, October 1). 83+ positive affirmations for spiritual protection (psychic energy). Manifest Like Whoa! https://manifestlikewhoa.com/positive-affirmations-spiritual-protection/

Avantika. (2020, December 23). 9 proven ways to protect yourself from psychic Attacks. BigBrainCoach. https://bigbraincoach.com/psychic-attacks/

Five ways to protect yourself from psychic attacks. (n.d.). Gaia https://www.gaia.com/article/protect-yourself-from-psychic-attacks

How to Create A Personal Energy Shield for Protection - abundance coach for women in business. (2022, February 23). Abundance Coach for Women in Business | Evelyn Lim. https://www.evelynlim.com/how-to-create-a-personal-energy-shield-for-protection/

How to smudge or hold a space clearing ceremony in your home. (2019, October 23). Glad.Is. https://glad.is/blogs/articles/how-smudge-or-hold-a-space-clearing-ceremony-in-your-home

Milazzo, N. (2022). Binaural Beats Research Analysis. https://examine.com/other/binauralbeats/

Original Products. (2021, May 18). Spiritual protection against psychic attacks. Original Botanica; www.originalbotanica.com#creator. https://originalbotanica.com/blog/spiritual-protection-against-psychic-attacks

Pawula, S. (2011, September 17). How to create a self-protective bubble —. Always Well Within. https://www.alwayswellwithin.com/blog/2011/09/18/vulnerability-and-protection

Peterson, K. (2020, September 5). Spiritual bath: DIY energy cleanse. Balance. https://www.balance-withus.com/blog/spiritual-bath-diy-energy-cleanse/

Sangimino, M. (2020, July 20). Meditation script: Protecting your energy. Soul & Sea. https://medium.com/soul-sea/meditation-script-protecting-your-energy-243d7929af3d

Tanaaz. (2015, March 11). 9 ways to protect yourself from psychic attacks. Forever Conscious. https://foreverconscious.com/9-ways-to-protect-yourself-from-psychic-attacks

The College of Psychic Studies : Enlighten : What is a psychic attack. (n.d.). The College of Psychic Studies. https://www.collegeofpsychicstudies.co.uk/enlighten/what-is-a-psychic-attack/

6 crystals to protect yourself from toxic people & negative energy. (2020, February 11). Mindbodygreen. https://www.mindbodygreen.com/articles/crystals-for-protection

9 powerful Air element crystals for inspiration. (2021, November 15). Crystals Alchemy. https://crystalsalchemy.com/air-element-crystals

9 powerful Earth element crystals for abundance. (2021, November 15). Crystals Alchemy. https://crystalsalchemy.com/earth-element-crystals

9 powerful Water element crystals for love and inner peace. (2021, November 17). Crystals Alchemy. https://crystalsalchemy.com/water-element-crystals

Darcy. (2022, August 4). Rune for protection – your guide for the meanings and use of Norse runes. Mythology Merchant. https://www.mythologymerchant.com/rune-for-protection-your-guide-for-the-meanings-and-use-of-norse-runes/

De Leonardis, K. (2022, May 3). 6 ways to energetically cleanse & protect your home – Lynn Hazan. Lynnhazan.com. https://lynnhazan.com/lifestyle/6-ways-to-energetically-cleanse-protect-your-home/

Fire Element Crystals: 9 best healing stones to balance your elements. (2021, November 14). Crystals Alchemy. https://crystalsalchemy.com/fire-element-crystals

Greenwood, C. (2021, December 10). 9 protection rituals to protect your space and energy. Outofstress.com. https://www.outofstress.com/protection-rituals/

Infusing folk magic into your home (with magical protection salt). (n.d.). Beccapiastrelli.com. https://beccapiastrelli.com/house-witchery/

Insight Network, Inc. (n.d.). Insight timer - #1 free meditation app for sleep, relax & more. Insighttimer.com. https://insighttimer.com/kathrynmccusker/guided-meditations/kundalini-mantra-meditation-aad-guray-nameh-protection

Johnson, E. (n.d.). 3 simple protection rituals. Zennedout.com. https://zennedout.com/3-simple-protection-rituals/

Kristenson, S. (2022, May 6). 60 protection affirmations to feel safe & secure. Happier Human; Steve Scott. https://www.happierhuman.com/protection-affirmations/

Michelle, H. (2017, August 12). Warding Ritual for Spiritual Protection of your Home. Witch on Fire. https://www.patheos.com/blogs/witchonfire/2017/08/warding-ritual-protection/

Rose, M. (2022, December 8). How to use protection magic: 5 spells that clear negative energy. StyleCaster. https://stylecaster.com/how-to-use-protection-magic/

Thorp, T. (2019, February 4). Guided meditation: Ground yourself using the Earth element. Chopra. https://chopra.com/articles/guided-meditation-ground-yourself-using-the-earth-element

Tim, & Marieke. (2020, February 1). Aad Guray Nameh - mantra for protection. Kundalini Yoga School. https://kundaliniyogaschool.org/2020/02/01/aad-guray-nameh-mantra-protection-kundalini-yoga/

Vialet B Rayne, C. (1566601033000). Archangels and their crystals. Linkedin.com. https://www.linkedin.com/pulse/archangels-crystals-vialet-b-rayne-crmt/

Wigington, P. (2009, July 5). Protection Magic. Learn Religions. https://www.learnreligions.com/magic-protection-spells-and-rituals-2562176

Minotra, T. (2022, July 5). 70+ powerful Affirmations for Protection & safety. ThediaryforLife. https://www.thediaryforlife.com/affirmations-for-protection-safety

15 signs you're having A Kundalini awakening + what it means. (2021, May 18). Mindbodygreen. https://www.mindbodygreen.com/articles/kundalini-awakening

Cuncic, A. (2019, May 29). How to practice Kundalini meditation. Verywell Mind. https://www.verywellmind.com/what-is-kundalini-meditation-4688618

Isaacs, N. (2021, May 4). Is a Kundalini awakening safe? Yoga Journal. https://www.yogajournal.com/yoga-101/types-of-yoga/kundalini/kundalini-awakening/

Kundalini meditation: Benefits, how to try, and dangers. (2020, August 18). Healthline. https://www.healthline.com/health/kundalini-meditation

Kundalini yoga 101: Everything you wanted to know. (2018, March 16). Mindbodygreen. https://www.mindbodygreen.com/articles/kundalini-yoga-101-everything-you-wanted-to-know

Kundalini: Awakening to the treasure within. (n.d.). Sadhguru.org. https://isha.sadhguru.org/us/en/wisdom/article/kundalini-awakening

Understanding the chakras and Kundalini energy. (n.d.). Art Of Living (India). https://www.artofliving.org/in-en/understanding-chakras-and-kundalini-energy

You are being redirected. (n.d.). Ananda.org. https://www.ananda.org/meditation/meditation-support/articles/awakening-kundalini

Made in the USA
Monee, IL
27 September 2024

66690174R00134